# Jim Cropper:
# The Dog Man

Dan in action on his feet with Jim at the Bodfari trial in 2004

as told to
# Edward Hart

with
contributions
from
Shirley Cropper
Tony Iley
Alf Kyme
Thomas Longton

Shirley with Bob at Deerplay

# Jim Cropper: The Dog Man

ISBN 1-85829-065-1

©2005

Printed by
Post Haste Printers
Pocklington
01759 306766

Thanks to:
Shirley Cropper
Gus Dermody
Tony Iley
Alf Kyme
and
Thomas Longton
for additional contributions.
Rosemary Cooper
for word processing.
Steven Townsend
for the Photo Album section.
Austin Bennett for the
picture of Jim at Deerplay
in the snow.

Typeset and published by WSN
5 Vale Crescent
Bishop Wilton
York
YO42 1SU
Tel 01759 368577
email workingsheepdog@hotmail.com
websites www.where2c.com and www.workingsheepdog.org
web page www.workingsheepdog.org/JimCropper.html

Alf, eager to go!

# Contents

Foreword 4

My Early Life 5

About Jim 7

A Day to Remember 13

Choosing & Training a Pup 15

Trialling 22

Judging 25

Shirley 29

Sheep Breeds 35

Practical Shepherding 37

Doubles 41

Great Dogs and Great Men 43

Difficult Dogs 47

Feeding 49

Auctions 50

Tour of the Trials 51

History of Trials 56

Overseas Trips 59

One Man and His Dog 62

Carving 67

At the End 69

Jim's Trials Successes 71

Useful Contacts 75

Pedigrees 77

Photo Album 83

About the Author 95

Bibliography 96

NOTES

• Except where otherwise stated, all lists of people and dogs depicted in photographs are in order, running left to right

• Where amounts are shown in pre decimal currency (£sd), 10s(hillings) is the equivalent of 50p; although worth considerably more nowadays!

# Foreword from Gus Dermody

In the mid 1960s I became involved in a whole new ball game - Sheepdog Trials. I was acting as "time keeper" at Macclesfield Sheep Dog Trials. It was midday, the sheep were awkward and, because there was no running order, there were no volunteers.

An old car came on to the field - out piled a young man with his family and dogs and immediately booked in two single and one brace runs. The young man was Jim Cropper. I had never met him before, only read about his trial results, so I was intrigued to see him compete. With minutes to spare, his three competitive runs were over and although he didn't win, he ended up in the prize list. As quickly as he came he was gone - off to another trial - and since then I have watched his progress with admiration for the practical way he shepherds sheep.

It doesn't matter whether it be a Nursery or World Trial, Jim puts everything into it. Many people are astounded how he can have a dog fully trained and competing in Nursery Trials at only 12 months.

You'll always see him positioned so he can see the field and, even when talking in a group of people, he will be glancing across at the running, not wanting to miss anything.

It doesn't matter whether it is a hill trial on rough ground or an extensive flat pasture, both he and his dogs are capable of taking the top prizes.

Quite often at a National or International trial the announcer asks if the people in the Grandstand will keep quiet whilst the competitors run their dogs. I've never heard this request when Jim walks to the post. It's a sign of a great handler when the whole grandstand falls so quiet that you could hear a pin drop.

Many top handlers reach their dizzy heights with one or two dogs in their lifetime but the mark of a really great sheepdog man is to get there with several: Cropper's Fleet; Cropper's Cap; Cropper's Sid and so on. With Bonnie and Clyde, Cap I and Cap II, Dan and Alf - all different yet all tremendous work and competition dogs.

A good "sheep man" in the Derbyshire Dales thought he could "read" sheep better than most, but I remember his telling me of watching a sheep dog trial whilst standing with Jim Cropper, who was virtually commentating on each run. Jim's ability to forecast what each ewe was likely to do was way way ahead of his. The "sheep man" classed it as an unfair advantage! Jim certainly studies sheep and knows just where to put the pressure on or off.

His ability to impart his knowledge to others is tremendous. I certainly had cause to thank him only nine months ago with a certain aspect of training. I'd asked other top people to no avail. Two minutes in Jim's training field had the problem solved - he made it look so easy.

Jims' wife, Shirley, has come a great distance in a short time - from Nursery Trials to the International in a few years with the same dog. This is living proof of Jim's ability and teaching skills.

I don't suppose many know of his artistic side. His stone carvings were the main prize in the 2004 "One Man and His Dog" series, and Jim, his brother, Stanley, and their father are all competent artists.

A lot of water has gone under the bridge since I first saw Jim. I never dreamt we would end up together commentating on the BBC "One Man and His Dog" programme, but he is a great asset and often puts forward a fresh view on what is being shown.

This is the book I have been wanting to read - it's been a long time coming - and I'm sure that readers will find it both informative and entertaining. It will probably end up as one of the main sheep dog books to stand the test of time.

# My early life

Straight out of a coal mine onto the hills

My early life was in the country, but not on a farm. My interest in farm dogs built slowly. Bert Riley had the land opposite my home, and I marvelled at the way he brought the sheep down from the hills. Bert's bitch had a litter of puppies, and I pestered my father to buy one for me.

However, that is jumping ahead. I was born in May 1941, the son of a miner. My father worked in a drift mine across the valley, and by dint of hard work had managed to acquire 30 acres of upland grass well over one thousand feet on the wet and windy west side of the Pennines.

This damp climate suited the cotton industry, which together with mining was the basic local industry. My mother was a weaver, and met my father near where we live now. In their courting days she walked from Wier village, while he walked from Dean, so each covered a couple of miles before they could meet. There weren't even any local cinemas to attend.

The first farm I lived on was called Harrow Stiles. We moved there, a mile uphill from Dean village, when I was five. It was a 30 acre farm, where my father kept 20 calves, some hens and pigs, but no sheep. This meant changing primary schools, from Water Primary to the Northern Primary, a two mile walk from the farmhouse. My father had a horse and cart, but he never took us to school, so I walked with my older brother Stanley and younger sister Yvonne. I was the only one to show a little interest in the livestock; I helped my mother feed the calves.

There was no water at Harrow Stiles, no gas and no electricity. We had no water because the local coal mines robbed us of most of the natural springs nearby, so we carried the water a quarter of a mile from the well of a neighbouring farm. We lived there for three years; I can remember the severe winters which toughened me up for a life of outdoor work.

We soon moved to a chip shop in Rawtenstall. This was for me like being in prison for a year and a half, until we moved back into the countryside, to a small terraced house in Dimockshaw. The house had mains water, gas and electricity, and, to my delight, a working farm just over the road. That was where I met Bert Riley the farmer. We moved again, back to Dean village, but I never forgot Bert working the Border Collie; this was forever imprinted on my brain.

At the age of 14 years, I at last got my first dog, a Border Collie called Lassie. She cost 10s, and by the time she was 8 months old, we had some hens in a pen which she would round up for me. At this stage I didn't know a great deal about training dogs, but I did learn a little. Lassie would lie down and go left and right. Sadly, she never got the chance to work on sheep.

Lassie moved with us to Turn Hill Farm. I was 16, and we had 40 dairy cattle which we milked by hand. Lassie would bring them in from the fields, but unfortunately one of the local farmers accidentally ran her over with his tractor.

Twelve months later we got about 50 sheep. I had an old stray dog called Laddie. Somebody had trained him at some point, because he knew how to round up cattle and sheep. This was very handy for me, and my father put me in charge of the sheep. Laddie taught me a lot by the way he worked.

By that time I had left school and was working

Stanley Earnshaw, with spectator Jim

in a drift mine, one of 30 men. The seams were between 18 inches and 3 feet high, the work anything but pleasant, but the pay quite good. I managed to buy some little fields. Then I managed to rent some land from the North West Water Board, which ran to 1475 feet.

There were 800 acres of this high-lying rough grazing. I struggled for the first two or three years, during which time I saw a black and white dog that worked wonderfully in the yards.

This dog sired a litter, and one pup was an absolute beauty, but was £7.10s. That was the equivalent of a week's wages and I couldn't afford it. My father was not much of a dog man, but he said: 'We'd better go and see him.' The sire, Rex, had a reputation for being one of the best of hill dogs. The deal was done.

Two years later, I knew I had something special. The dog was housed in a pen with sides 12 to 14 feet high, but he wanted to get out to a bitch in season, and climbed a ladder like a chap.

I worked him around my sheep at home, learning all the time. Then one day my neighbour told me there was a nursery sheepdog trial nearby.

I didn't know what even a small trial was, but we walked down over the hills. I was hooked.

Ernest Dawson, Len Greenwood and John Heap were there. They talked and talked, trying to persuade me to run. 'No', I kept saying. 'My dog can't drive.' Finally they persuaded me to run, and Bob Moore helped teach me to drive. I watched as many dogs at as many trials as I could find in the neighbourhood.

There was a trial at Tern Hill, Dean Lane, on some Water Board land. This was in 1964, and I ran Rex, the unregistered dog I had got after Laddie, and was placed second on my first outing. Then I was first at Holme-in-Cliviger, fifth at Meltham, and third at Holme-in-Cliviger. I had got the bug.

A friend, Billy Newell, told me he was going to the 1964 International at York, and would take me along. Herbert Worthington won with Juno. That level turf at York Knavesmire, of horseracing fame, was of course completely different from the rugged, wet hills that were my home. Of particular interest to me was Tot Longton, running Rob, then 18 months, and destined to become one of the steadiest and most thoughtful dogs on the circuit.

Then Tom Bonella ran a dog called Ben. On my return I saw he had advertised in Scottish Farmer a litter by Bathgate's Rock. I wrote immediately, and had a letter back, saying he would send a pup to Waterfoot Station for £20 plus 10s carriage.

This dog was Fleet. A big, flashy, black and white dog, he was entered for Nurseries and won 23 awards including eight firsts in 21 trials. He was a large dog who would die for me. He also herded cattle, but got his eye knocked out. Knowing what I do now, I should never have put a dog of his quality on suckler cows. Sorry, Fleet, you really established me in those early days.

Fleet would work on his own and adjust to different types of sheep.

Tony Iley lived next door. He is another in the line of shepherd poets, and loved sheepdog work. We spent many a summer evening practising with our dogs, and talking pedigrees.

In 1967 and 1968 I was improving. I ran Cass (named after boxer Cassius Clay) and Fleet at Lowgill.

Fleet was twice English Driving Champion. I attended many trials with Tony Iley, and made the English team for the first time in 1968.

Fleet was by this time much in demand as a stud dog, and was very prepotent, his pups tending to have his best points and his striking markings.

In 1968 and 1969 I sent for two pups from the same breeding as Fleet. These were Bonnie and Clyde, named after the characters in the film. In their first season, they had 16 placings including eight victories. They made their mark at ten and eighteen months old and continued to impress.

I've always liked running young dogs. Others prefer a friend they can trust never to let them down, but I prefer the challenge of bringing on new blood all the time. There is no right and wrong at stake here; each to his own.

# About Jim
# - from Tony Iley

Amongst the shooting party, holding the guns, are Jim (wearing the long light coat) and Tony Iley (right)

It was at a trial somewhere in Yorkshire. Jim was running the young Fleet in one of his first trials. Fleet gathered and lifted the Swale ewes perfectly. Down the course he came, never deviating from the line and in perfect control. A good turn led onto the drive, accomplished with style and presence. The sheep came straight through the hurdle and this set up a tight turn onto the crossdrive. It was a run to remember, but then one of the Swale sinners turned, looked at Fleet and ran straight at him with intent. The young dog stood perfectly still, turned his head slightly to the side, opened his mouth and closed it on the grey nose. There was no aggression - just steely determination. The ewe spun on its heels and obediently joined the other two to complete the drive and walk straight into the pen. Forty nine and a half points out of fifty. We all saw it. Fleet's illustrious career had started with a bang.

That wasn't, however, the first time I had seen Jim. A couple of years earlier he had offered to put on a nursery trial at Turn Hill farm. I was on the committee of the Holme Sheepdog Trials Association and they had asked me to timekeep so that I could learn how to judge. The judge that day was Teddy Hullah, an ancient sheep and dog enthusiast. Teddy didn't have any recognisable system of judging. At the end of each run, he just plucked a score out of the air. Jim was running Rex that day. Rex was the king of the working machines but trialling was not his scene. Rex didn't get many points on the day, but Teddy's venom was reserved for "eye dogs". One poor dog that had completed the course, even though it was almost paying ground rent for time spent on its belly, got no points at all. "It wasn't worth anything", said Teddy.

Rex was a giant amongst work dogs and I'm not easily impressed. He had a brain to match his stamina and speed. I often saw him retrieve a turnip that Jim had thrown onto a pile of many hundreds. Even when he was prevented from watching, he could get the right one every time.

By now, I was living next door to Jim at Turn Hill cottage and we were training dogs at every opportunity. One day we took Fleet up to Lennie Greenwood's Ramsden farm. There was a really tough hill by the house. Lenny said "There aren't many dogs that will go up that". Jim said "This one will", and he did - straight up in one.

Turn Hill was an exciting place to live. From time to time, subsidence would cause holes to appear suddenly in the road. Holes big enough to swallow a car some of them were.

It could be a bit scary driving home at night. One Saturday night, Jim asked me to baby sit for him. I had a date that night so said no. When I returned home I found that Jim and his babysitter had been in disagreement with a man from the village who had shot the pair of them with his twelve bore shotgun. Only in Rossendale! A few days later, when I visited Jim in hospital, he showed me the wound in his upper thigh. "Good job it wasn't six inches higher or I'd be a wether" said Jim in typical fashion. Our kids got considerable entertainment many years later as Jim showed them the pellets still lodged in his leg.

Every so often I used to ring Jim, put on my best Scottish accent and pretend to be the great Jim Wilson wanting to buy Fleet. It worked for a time till Jim got wise and played along with it. I then tried a Welsh accent and became Alan Jones, the 1961 International Champion, again wanting to buy Fleet. Eventually both of these great men did ring to buy him and were no doubt perplexed by Jim going into a great spiel in Scottish or Welsh, thinking it was me again.

Then came Bonnie and Clyde. Bonnie was classy, fast and pliable. Clyde was powerful and unforgiving, but what a pair! The year Jim ran them in doubles at the Nationals there was a motion that dogs under two years old would not be eligible to compete. Tot Longton stood up at the meeting that night and said that, if the proposal had been in effect, we would not have seen the best doubles run that anyone could remember. He was right. The motion wasn't passed.

I eventually moved up to Scotland to shepherd in Dumfriesshire and became very friendly with Jock Richardson. I asked him to come down to Lancashire with me one weekend and judge a trial at Old Barn farm, Hapton. After the trial, we stayed the night with Jim. As the evening wore on, conversation came round to horses. Jock had been a keen horseman in his younger days and had led a stallion round the district to serve the local mares. Jim said that he had a good horse and Jock asked to see it. Jim requested Linda, his daughter, to get the horse. She disappeared into the night and some time later, hooves were heard trotting down the hall. Linda rode the horse into the living room, round the settee three times and out into the night again. Jock agreed it was a good horse!

Some years later, Jim rang me. He had a good dog that had got a bit sick of trialling. By now, I was shepherding at Dunsdale in the Cheviot Hills and Jim wanted me to take Cap and give him some everyday work. The first time I ran him, I thought he was going to finish up over the Scottish border - he was such an outrunner. He worked very hard for me on the Cheviots for a while. I never tried to do any trial work with him and in fact wondered whether he would be capable of getting back into trial mode. Jim took him away but returned to Northumberland with him to compete at the National a couple of months later. The night before the National, we took Cap up to my lambing field, a big rough piece of fenced-in hill about 200 acres in size. Cap ran like a dream, he answered every whistle and responded to every intonation, producing speed, care, half flanks or full flanks as Jim requested. I knew that he would win the National the next day and he did.

Well, it's a long time since the story began - some forty years in fact. It all started with three young men - Jim, David Carlton and myself - all debating who would be the first to stand on the bales at an International trial and who would be the first to win it. I suppose even then we all thought it would be Jim. We've all stood on the bales but the end of the story is still to be written.

# from Alf Kyme

Alf Kyme has known Jim all his life. 'They broke the mould when Jim Cropper was born', he said. 'There isn't another like him'.

'Whether working among sheep, training dogs, doing a repair job, standing in front of a crowd as a public speaker or training novice handlers, Jim is the tops', said Alf Kyme. 'He is big and powerful, yet remarkably precise in fine work like painting and sculpting. He is also one of the untidiest people I ever met. In his bachelor days he would be surrounded in his kitchen by a ring of coffee cups, because he hadn't bothered to wash any up.'

Alf Kyme is a keen sheep dog trainer now that he is retired. He lives at the well named Higher Walls Farm, Lumb, Rossendale, a few miles from Jim's home. He has a splendid collection of shepherds' crooks and walking sticks which he is pleased to show to visitors. His wife Barbara runs a bed-and-breakfast sideline, popular with competitors at the Deerplay sheep dog trials.

Alf recommends the Islands trials off Scotland's west coast, where a very pleasant week may be spent sailing from one trial to the next.

# from John Atkinson

**Jim Cropper, The People's Champion**

I have been aware of Jim Cropper ever since I first started trialling nearly 30 years ago. He didn't know me then, and I didn't know him, as it takes time to associate with each other in the world of sheepdogs. No animal ever goes charging in. It takes time. Sniffing about, not making eye contact, watching each other; that is how it is, and should be. Over time we have recognised each other, and have become good friends. He has visited my home and I his. We have talked about our lives and experiences and so formed a friendship. I have always seen Irwell House Farm as a high spot, where the wind from the Pennine Hills blows cold and hard, and despite being close to the towns of Burnley and Bacup, in Lancashire, England, one gets the feeling of remoteness when driving into the yard. This is the home of Jim Cropper. Born in Rossendale in the year 1941 Jim was the second child of a family of seven, for as well as his parents, he had three other brothers and a sister. Not from as expected, farming stock, Jim's father was an entrepreneur and had purchased a coal mine, so Jim spent his early days down the mine; sometimes working in tunnels only three feet high which tapered to eighteen inches. Five hours was the maximum working in such conditions, so as soon as Jim came to the surface, he was gone walking the hills and taking in the fresh air and open space. His father must have seen where his son's heart was, for as well as purchasing some land, he was also successful in renting a thousand acre farm from the local Water Board. It was stocked with sheep and Jim was told to go and look after it. He was a natural with stock and as well as making a success of the venture it also introduced him to using sheepdogs to help him with the management of such a vast grazing area. For this is high rugged hill country which brings with it harsh conditions.   Although Jim could always work a dog, trialling had not taken his attention until he first saw a trial in the next Dale to where he lived. After watching the trial from a distance, he thought that he could do just as well as the shepherds and sheep farmers competing. The dog he had at the time was a dog called Rex which he had purchased at the age of ten months for just £7. He had trained Rex to a good standard and at his very first trial in 1964 he took second place. He went on to take several awards that season and so became the start of a great success story. Big success came in the 1966/67 Nursery season, when, with an eighteen month old dog named Fleet, he took 23 awards from just 31 trials which included 8 wins. Fleet also had much success in the Opens, and must be one of if not the only dog ever to take two open wins in one day at two different venues with full pointed runs at both trials. Their success continued for, in 1973 along with his kennel mate Clyde, they won the International Supreme Brace Championship at Bala. At the same Championship, Jim was also placed Reserve Supreme Champion with Clyde in the Singles. Jim's success continued, winning numerous trials throughout the UK including many of the majors. Then in 1987 with a dog named Cap he took the English National Championship after finishing runner up the year before. The following year along with Cap, there was Cap ll with whom Jim took the Brace title on the BBC Television programme "One Man and His Dog". This is a programme I believe the Croppers have become prominent in, for in 1990 Katy Cropper, Jim's previous wife, won the title; then only last year, his current wife, Shirley Cropper, also took the title. I understand they are the only two women to have ever won this prestigious award, which gives me to believe that you first have to marry Jim Cropper to get it !!    It has to be said that

throughout his years Jim has been no angel and has gained something of a reputation as a wild boy who still carries the buckshot down one side of his body from a family feud.

Jim lives next door to a renowned public drinking house at the top of Deerplay Hill. It is known as the Deerplay Inn. One day Jim heard the tenancy was coming up and being a bit of an entrepreneur took it on " It's like putting Dracula in charge of a blood bank." was the word, but Jim made a reasonable success of it, but gave up the tenancy  a few years later; and concentrated on his sheep farming and dog training. He now has increased his flock to over a thousand ewes and his current farm extends to a thousand acres, which includes Deerplay Hill. This is where the famous Deerplay Hill Trial is held. It is notorious for being a dog leveller, due to the difficult terrain and the half mile gathers in the double lift final. However even though each competitor is only allowed to run one dog, it always attracts a very large entry.   Whether it is the influence of his new wife Shirley, a great girl with her feet on the ground, his maturing years, or just the decision to slow the pace down; Jim has changed into the "new" Jim Cropper. His drinking has finished, he has changed from his wild nights, to dining out with Shirley on a regular basis, and remains a kind caring person who will help anyone should they need his help. It is great to see, for to me he is one of, if not the best, handlers in England; and has so much to offer the sport. His knowledge of dog handling is unbelievable, and should he give you any tips on trialling, then it is best to listen in silence, for they will be words of great wisdom.

Jim is currently the most successful triallist in England, if not the UK He has become very difficult to beat. Few people can match his skill of handling on a trials course. Although it has to be said that the Longton family have been and are still the most acknowledged people in the sheepdog world, I know that Jim is a match for them. The reason they win so much is because they do it correctly. They do not cut corners , they do not think the judge is a plonker, they run as if they were judging. If things go wrong, they get it together and correct it, and continue as if they were winning. No chin hits the floor, only positive thinking. I admire such focus, for it makes winners. Jim should be given more praise in the the UK than is currently the case.   In 2004, Jim and his team of dogs were unbeatable, for from April to August he had 22 Open wins with Sid, (14) Mac, (4) Dan (3) and Alf (1).  He was winning numerous trials and in 2003 he was runner up to Aled Owen in the World Championship Sheepdog Trials, with his dog Sid. I did not attend the trial, so I cannot personally comment; but as always in trials there has been much discussion as to who should have really won. For although he was not given the title by the judges, he certainly was by the people watching. A true Peoples' Champion.

• You can visit John's website at www.whiterosesheepdogs.com

# from Thomas Longton

Thomas Longton and Mirk await their turn to run at a Lakeland trial.

One day, many moons ago, it was 3.00 am in the morning when I was awakened by a car arriving in the yard. It was the still of the night but the dogs were barking, they realised that they were going to a trial even though it was an early start.

Jim Cropper had arrived to travel with my Dad. It was extremely early to set out to a sheepdog trial but the event was in the Vale of Evesham in Worcestershire. Dad had to get up early as Jim was always on time. Maybe Jim had never been to bed! I think they had planned to arrive in Worcester for the 7.00 am start so they could run their dogs and then travel to the other end of the country up to Penrith in Cumbria for another trial. Such was their determination to go to trials, even when travelling was much slower then.

My Dad really loved to go to the trials with Jim because he was such good company. He kept Dad entertained on the long distances they travelled with his jokes, singing and endless conversation. Dad also knew that Jim was an exceptionally talented handler and very capable of scoring maximum points if the sheep were half decent at any trial. There was always a great mutual respect between them of their natural ability and competitive spirit at the trials. They travelled far and wide together and it always amazed but also reassured me how such opposites attracted. My Dad was teetotal and Jim quite the reverse! The common bond was the love of sheepdog trialling. As a family we all looked forward to hearing not only the results of the day but hearing Dad tell us about the laughs they had shared.

When I was younger, I was not interested in sheepdog trials as I thought it an old man's game! I used to travel with Dad, however, to local trials and I enjoyed the Royal Lancashire Show trial at Stanley Park in Blackpool the most, as, on sunny days, all the spectators could eat lunch whilst seated on a sunny bank. I remember watching Jim work with Fleet and how the dog used to work without seeming to do anything. All the other dogs ran all over the field and Fleet just needed to turn his head to move the sheep. Fleet was a very special dog.

Jim has been lucky throughout the years in having several exceptional dogs which have given him much success on the trials fields. I have learned so much by watching Jim handle his dogs over the years and most recently, over the last ten years, he has improved the level of handling at trials and raised the bar for all the other competitors to aim for. He still leads the way. He has gained recognition and success and it is extremely sad that, to date, a Supreme or World title has not accompanied this incredible unmatchable talent.

Jim has always been willing to help anyone, young or old, with helpful advice when they are struggling with any aspect of training or handling their dog. I have also enjoyed watching the progress of Shirley. It has been great to see how she has improved with the help of Jimmy. Now, when they both go to trials, you have both Croppers to contend with. It is a great credit to her that she has represented England at the International trials and it is not that she has merely had luck on her side - she is consistently good and never far from the prize list.

Over the last few years, Jim has been the one to watch at all the trials as it is enlightening to see him handle his dogs and fantastic how he reads the sheep. He has a lifetime's history of working with sheep and it amazes me how his very young dogs are so well trained and seem already to have the experience of an older dog despite their tender years.

Jim's larger than life presence brightens up the dullest of days. He has always been able to laugh and joke, even when the trialling is not going so well. We enjoy the English National trials now, not only for the competition, but also for the caravan life that Jim and Shirley now share. Jim was introduced to this way of life when Shirley bought his "bunk bed on wheels". We have laughed so much about the time that Jim's bed collapsed in the night and he was rigged like a sheep and shouting for Shirley to get him up. Apart from the fact that the caravan door is not wide enough for Jim to walk through face on, it is almost as good as the headquarters hotel!!

Noone is better known throughout the world of sheepdogs than is Jim, and he has thoroughly deserved the acclamation of the Wilkinson Sword Trophy.

• Thomas and Anne Longton have recently converted a barn into a luxurious holiday spot. For details of 'The Shepherd's Barn', where you can combine a holiday with sheepdog training, visit www.longtonsheepdogs.com or ring 01524 36867.

Tot Longton

Jim with Fleet and Bill Little wih Jock at a trial in the mid 1960s, planning a trip to J M Wilson in Scotland

# A day to remember

One day in 1966, a letter arrived out of the blue that was to change my whole life. The legendary Jim Wilson, who won eight ISDS Supreme Championships, had read about Fleet, whose dam was sired by Jim's Whitehope Bill. At that time Fleet had 23 placings, including eight firsts; he was only unplaced once or twice. It was a record that was to remain unbeaten until I did so with Sid in 2000.

'I'm getting a bit old, and suffering from arthritis, and I'd like to see Fleet. Could you manage to bring him up?' wrote Jim Wilson. It was like receiving a royal command.

At the next trial I discussed the letter with Bill Little. 'We could have a look up, and see Bathgate's Rock at the same time', he said. He also hoped to call on John Richardson, and see Wiston Cap.

They all lived in the Peebles area of the Scottish Borders, at that time a country of lovely, rolling green hills before those dreadful and wasteful conifers blanketed the countryside.

Bill Little lived at Goosnargh, 35 miles away. He arranged everything, including picking me up at 3 a m in his little Mini. He and I squashed into the front, the back seat having been taken out to accommodate Fleet and Bill's dog, Jock.

We drove through Burnley to Settle, and picked up the M6 near Kirby Lonsdale. We passed through Moffat, with its sculpture of a Blackface ram. The story goes that the sculptor had missed the ears off the sheep, which so devastated him that he took his own life.

Our first port of call was Manor Water, Peebles, where we saw Rock run, and inspected some young dogs. It was no great distance to Whitehope, where Jim Wilson was waiting for us in a 20 acre field. He had an old Land Rover with an open back, just low sides and no top. There were five dogs in the back, sitting quietly, not tied in. They must have come a few miles by road like that.

Their owner said: 'I've been looking forward to seeing Fleet run', and had a bunch of a dozen Blackface ewes ready, some 500 yards away. Jim Wilson was in the top bracket with his Blackfaces as well as with his dogs.

I had a run with Fleet. I couldn't get my dog anywhere near those wild sheep. There I stood, yelling and bawling, and feeling a like a complete amateur. Finally I made some sort of a show, and Jim said he was very impressed with Fleet. The merest vestige of a smile on his face told me that I had not made the best job of running a dog. Then Bill Little followed, and did much the same. He didn't seem to get his dog in contact with that touchy little flock.

All this time Jim's own dogs were in the back of the Land Rover, which was parked 30 or 40 yards away at such an angle that they could watch every move – and they did. 'I'll run you Bill', said their owner, following this up by calling 'Bill' in a very low voice. The dog immediately hopped out, and none of the others stirred. Had they been my dogs, I knew that the lot would have cascaded to the ground, and would have had to be put back again. Jim Wilson had already impressed me with his quiet authority and mild manner.

The sheep were again in a bunch, 500 yards away. With Bill the dog at his side, he gave the gentlest of whistles through his teeth. His dog circled the sheep, and began to bring them towards us. Jim Wilson was talking throughout, but seemed to command the dog through the tone of his voice rather than different words.

He would say 'Bill!' in several tones, all of which met with an instant response from the dog. To go to the right he would say 'Bill Bill'; to the left he would repeat 'Biiiil Biiiil' in a long drawn out voice.

Here was I, who had been winning Nursery trials all over the north of England, standing with this experienced Scot, and realising that I knew nothing. The way Bill got to his sheep, lifted them, and glided them around the field was an absolute eye opener. The dog was just full of class under such a highly professional shepherd.

'I'll show you a dog that will win the International!', said Jim Wilson. Bill III was out of Fly, dam of Wiston Cap. This forecast proved correct when David McTier handled Bill for Jim Wilson, bringing the latter's Supreme Championship titles to nine in Kilmartin in 1970.

After this dog demonstrated his potential, he was told to 'Get Back In', and was replaced by another of the five, all of which seemed to work like peas in a pod. These dogs were waiting and watching, but the remarkable thing was that they were not at all on edge. All remained in the open vehicle, quite relaxed. The demonstration proceeded for an hour, by the end of which I was feeling about two feet tall, and believing that I knew nothing about either sheep or dogs.

I took in everything I could, knowing that I was in the presence of a master, one of the pioneers of sheep dog handling in a cool, quiet fashion. Bill Little and I talked about it all the way home.

Before that, we had moved on to John Gilchrist's at Roslyn, near Peebles, where we had tea and home-baked scones. John ran the immortal Spot, a top class hill dog and a top class trials dog. Gilchrist's Spot was a name to conjure with, a great dog that raised the standard of the Border Collie through his many excellent progeny. The fact that his sheep were half a mile away meant nothing to that dog.

Finally, we visited John (Jock) Richardson at Lyne. By now it had got rather late in the day, and we did not see a lot of the legendary Wiston Cap. This was a pity because Wiston Cap was the outstanding dog of his time.

I saw John Richardson win the International with Wiston Cap at Cardiff in 1965. His handling was top class. His whistle sent Cap up a gear, or down a gear, as the case merited. It was just like watching a well-oiled machine changing gear. Wiston Cap was a tall, handsome black and white with a lovely style and carriage, emblazoned for all to see as the emblem of the International Sheep Dog Society.

Not only was Cap a great dog, but he proved a tremendous sire. 'WistonCappers' became a common feature of the trials scene, to the point where Tim Longton in 'The Sheep Dog: Its Work and Training', written with Edward Hart, suggested that another line was needed.

Wiston Cap was used so much that sheep dog handlers, a fanciful bunch at the best of times, suggested that the new M6 through Cumbria was being constructed to facilitate the passage of English bitches to Wiston Cap north of the border!

When Jock Richardson walked to the stake with Wiston Cap, all went very still. The grandstand was hushed, spectators around the ground concentrated on the black and white dog about to glide away into the distance. I've no doubt that the judges became extra alert.

We returned home to Lancashire about 3 am, 24 hours after we set off. It was the sort of day we took in our stride, but on reflection, what a background for lifelong memories! John Gilchrist and Spot, John Bathgate and Rock, Jim Wilson and his five, Jock Richardson and Wiston Cap all in one day! I can only feel deeply thankful that I was in the right place at the right time.

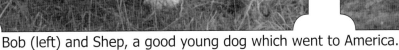

# Choosing a Pup

Bob (left) and Shep, a good young dog which went to America.

I've been to thousands and thousands of trials and no two are ever alike. The sheep are all different. They might be wild, stiff, stubborn or stupid. They might be 'heavy' - the dog man's term for those, usually big, sheep like Suffolk tups that need a tough dog to move them. You'll not find Suffolk tups at a trial, but it's the sort fitting the 'heavy' description.

The course can be steep, flat, undulating, rushy, hillocky, wide or narrow. The weather can be hot, still, blowing a gale or raining cats and dogs. There might be patches of mist that lift and return. There might be hard frost or snow.

All these variables mean that, to win trials consistently, you need a dog that is brainy and adaptable. You must look well into the breeding. A dog is born with those characteristics, but if they are absent you can't put them there. I have to pass quite a lot of dogs through my hands before I find one that has all that is needed.

Dogs vary enormously. Dan was a big, leggy, gangling sort of dog at seven months, but very brainy and intelligent. He was winning trials at eleven months. His kennel mate, Alf, took longer to train, and was more difficult. He was coming up to two years old before he accomplished anything, but became a very good dog.

Take note of the parents, but be prepared to go back several generations. If there is a sprinkling of international competitors, so much the better. Check for any hereditary faults such as hip dysplasia, eye trouble or undershot jaw.

I like smooth coated dogs. My wife Shirley prefers rough coated ones. It is purely a matter of personal preference. My favourites are black and white, or black, white and tan. I am not so keen on red dogs. Sheep seem to stare at them rather than respond, and I have seen a fox pass among sheep that simply kept on grazing. I like the ears to be set on top, but not necessarily prick-eared. Droopy or spaniel-eared dogs are to be avoided.

If you buy a pup from the litter, eight weeks is about the right age. I usually buy a pup at between ten weeks and six months, before anyone else has messed it about.

Pups should be attentive. I like one that will listen to me; a bold pup that comes straight up and wants to be a pal. Yet other people may like the quiet ones that sit back and weigh up the situation. I defy anyone to pick a winner from the nest. They can change so much.

A pup should be neither too aggressive nor too shy. The main thing is that it must be trainable. Its nature is much affected by its upbringing. It is wise for a pup to be taken out as much as possible. Mine are reared in open runs some eight or ten yards long. They have grass runs, which are better for the feet than wood, brick or concrete, which tend to spread the feet. Grass pulls up the knuckles, with wood the next best.

Temperament is very important. A dog is no good today if it won't stand noise. There is so much noise in the world, and sheepdog trials may be staged near a noisy fairground, or as an adjunct to a show that has noisy items such as motorcycles.

A trials dog in particular must be able to mix with people. This is a mixture of inherited characteristics and upbringing. When any children come here, the first thing they do is take the pups out.

Overshot jaw

Undershot jaw

Bad tail

Knock knees

Flat footed

Correct

Down on its hocks

Bad ears: spaniel ears

Good ears

Bad ears: crossed ears

Badly bow legged

Bad hocks: Cow hocked

Good posture

Some things to avoid when choosing a pup, drawn by Jim

Socialising Shirley's young dogs (Lilly, Bob, Roy and Mac) are the kids (Charlie, Sophie and Chloe).

# Socialising Pups

This has to be done at home, after the pups have been wormed and injected at approximately ten weeks old. Children come up to the farm and take the pups out for little gentle walks. Also at this age a "call back" whistle can be introduced to a young dog. For example, when feeding the pups a calling whistle will bring them to the food. Later in life the same whistle can be used to call the dog off the sheep when half a mile away.

Never do we socialise pups at trials. This only winds them up. They will hear too many whistles and travelling can be physically upsetting. Pups should always be allowed to play outside in large pens. Our grandchildren and nieces, Sophie, Charlie and Chloe, are 13 years old and love to visit the farm. They take all the young dogs out for a walk on the hills. Sophie and Chloe both have a dog of their own and enjoy helping with and training the dogs. They have been doing this since they were nine years old. There are many tasks they love to do such as helping with lambing, shearing and the training of the young pups. Almost every weekend they go up to the farm, clean up and feed the dogs and socialise the pups and nervous dogs. All the dogs are walked by them. These activities widen the pup's experiences, getting them ready to be trained later on.

At the Deerplay Trial the two girls help with the letting out and sometimes gather the whole flock in the morning ready for the trial.

Lambing season is the busiest time of the year and help is needed from anyone who is on hand. Sophie and Chloe get up early in the morning and, from 5 to 6 am they go with me or on their own around the flock of ewes. If they find any sheep struggling to give birth they catch it and, with the experience they have picked up from watching me, they deliver the lamb with no hassle at all. Other lambing problems such as neglected lambs are easily sorted out.

Shearing is another job where help is always needed and they give assistance along with the rest of the shearers and friends. They put the wool into the sacks that are being sent off to Bradford. As there are over 600 sheep to clip in one day, it is a long and usually hot affair.

Sophie and Chloe worm the sheep and help Jim to feed them in winter. They will all be out for hours on the quad in blistering sunshine or freezing bitter winds. Watching me and Shirley work on the farm teaches them things they have never done in their life. When the sheep are being gathered with the most experienced dogs, they both have their eyes glued to what is going on and they hope that their own dogs will be as good as mine and Shirley's in the future.

The two girls attend many different trials and shows with their uncle and aunt. Travelling all over the country to trials is a very enjoyable way of gaining experience of the things the shepherd must do during his or her day to day life. Watching the trials that are held at the farm is also one of their favourite pastimes. When they and their dogs are more experienced, they hope to go on to win trophies and medals as we have done.

With trials in mind, you must be that bit more careful than when choosing an ordinary working dog. Remember the standards are now very high, and a lot of people are knocking on the door, trying to make the National team.

My old friend Lennie Greenwood bred a litter every year, and simply kept the one that was left after the others had had their pick. He always had good dogs, which indicated that it is the trainer as much as anything.

The pup needs a good bellyful of the right food, and plenty of exercise on grass and soil (see chapter on Feeding).

**The First Steps**
There is work to be done before the young dog sees any sheep. The first step is to isolate the dog from the gang in which it has grown up. It would be altogether too giddy if left in the pack. From now on it will be in a one-to-one situation with the trainer as pack leader. This is essential. It must look to its trainer, and not to other dogs. If a pup does not respond, a few days in a darker room should suffice to bring it round. It must be pleased to see you, and so become submissive.

Common sense plays a big part in sheepdog training. Every dog is different, and every handler is different. It is therefore a mistake to lay down too many hard and fast rules.

I know I'm lucky when it comes to early handling of a pup. When you are single handed, you must put a collar on your pup, making sure it can't be slipped, and lead it about. I hand over to my grandchildren and Shirley's nieces, who all love being among puppies. Both parties benefit!

Put on the leather collar for the first time as tight as ever you dare without cutting off the air supply. One finger between collar and neck

suffices. The pup may howl and scream and throw itself about, but will soon realise that all its efforts are to no avail. Two hours is long enough for this first session. but do keep an eye on it.

Before the dog is introduced to sheep, it must be taught to lead. A length of light nylon cord is attached to the trainee's collar after it has learnt not to bite or chew. Nylon washing lines as bought at a supermarket do fine.

Two vital points must be made. On no account must the pup be allowed to slip its lead, or to bite through it. If it succeeds on either of these counts, it will always be looking for another chance. When you come to tie it up, use a light chain. A rope may be bitten through, starting a lifetime of trouble. Fasten the lead to a secure ring in a smooth brick wall the first time the pup is tied up.

Then untie the dog and take it for a walk. This is seldom difficult if the initial tying up has been done properly. Once the pup has accepted the collar, it may be slackened a notch. Talk encouragingly to the pup. If it tries to pull ahead, give a good yank and say "Come In Here! Carry a stick, because the dog must become accustomed to one, but do not use it for any more than a slight tap on the nose if it continues to try to forge ahead. You sometimes see dogs dragging their handlers around, and this is very bad manners.

The pup must learn to lie down, stay down and come to heel. Start by pressing the pup kindly but firmly onto the ground, saying 'Lie Down' in a firm voice. This should not be too difficult if the dog is thoroughly accustomed to its collar and lead. A few lessons should suffice.

The usual command to return to the handler is 'That'll Do!' Be sure to make a fuss of the pup when it does so. If it is stubborn, pull on the rope a few times. Do not carry on these exercises for very long, and certainly not until the dog gets fed up with them.

Some dogs get worked up in the early stages, but firmness and patience in these should win the day. Wife and kiddies are extremely useful in these early stages! I have spent all this time discussing what to do and the dog has not even seen sheep! It may seem tedious, but is absolutely vital, and if you neglect these stages you may well have to come back to them later.

**Introducing to sheep**
You are now ready to see if the pup is showing an interest in sheep. I think six months is the ideal age to find out whether the dog has any eye for

sheep. It is at the most receptive, and to wait till the dog is twelve to eighteen months old, means you lose a lot of its potential working life, which is brief enough by human standards. Remember we are harnessing the hunting instincts of a young dog, and wild dogs or wolves have to learn to fend for themselves at six months. Not everyone appreciates this analogy, but it is a true one.

All this goes back to animal instincts. As pack leader you have to make the hunting instinct work for you. Remember, a Border Collie in the wrong hands can become a sheep killer.

Once again I emphasise that no two dogs are alike. Some may need a lot of encouragement - what we call very 'light' dogs. Others may exhibit the killer instinct to a marked degree. Your dog is still on the lead, and can be given harsh words if it goes in for the kill. Combine that with tightening the line to prevent it actually gripping the sheep. Unchecked, this dog would have wool all over the place at best, and actual physical injuries or death at the worst. On the trials field the gripper gets no second chance. 'Thank you Mr Cropper', would be the judges' immediate reaction!

There is a very fine line between correcting a gripping tendency and stopping the working instinct altogether. Some dogs have a terrific amount of herding and killer instinct, so how should this be dealt with? My method is to use the lungeing whip as is common in horse circles. It has a short stock and a thong up to ten feet long. I'm a pretty good shot with it, and can crack it just in front of the dog's nose. It's a skill worth acquiring. The object is NOT to strike the dog; the thong lands just in front of its nose. That is a reminder of the similarity between horse and dog training. A young horse that slips its headcollar or breaks its halter will be trying to repeat the dodge for the rest of its life. It must on no account be allowed to get away, and the same applies to a dog slipping its collar or biting through its lead.

Some trainers use a tightly folded plastic bag, using it to strike just in front of the dog. The main thing is to stop the grip and regain the dog's attention.

The sheep used in training a pup play a big part. You must not use tups (rams), ewes in-lamb, or weak sheep. Geld sheep, or hoggs before their first mating, are ideal. They can't do damage either to themselves or the dog, whereas a hammering from a strong tup could put a pup off working for life.

You will probably have to make do with whatever field is available, but there are certain basic rules. The field must not be too large; one or two acres is plenty big enough. Ten acres is far too large. In recent years trainers have developed a circular pen, and this is ideal. It has no corners into which the sheep can attempt to hide, and five feet tall sides which discourage any attempt to jump out.

It is now possible to buy five foot netting, but if you prefer, two rolls of sheep netting, one above the other, will suffice. If the stronger pig netting is used, don't forget that the small squares go to the bottom, not to the top as I've seen County Council workers do!

The whole pen is finished with a wooden rail on top. This strengthens the structure, and is something for the animals to look at. The main point is that they must on no account escape. Sheep soon find any weak point in a pen, and then wreck it. Tempers flare, and the whole session is wasted.

If you cannot immediately rise to this type of pen, make sure there are no traps, shelters or bad corners. A wide hedge is something for the sheep to hide under, so fence it off, and fence across an awkward corner.

Take the dog on a long lead for its first encounter with sheep. It must not be allowed to dash forward. Jerk it back if necessary, and keep it there using a light wand in front of its face. You wouldn't let your children dash through a gate in front of you; apply the same to the dog, and let it know who is in charge.

Don't bother with the STOP whistle until the dog is working the sheep nicely. When it halts of its own accord, then give it the STOP whistle or say LIE DOWN! Don't use the word unnecessarily. It is a case of perpetually taking out the dog, two or three times a day if possible, and only for five or ten minutes.

If the dog starts eating muck, or not bothering with the sheep, or yawning or sniffing about, give up for the day. The dog has to want to work, but be sure to praise it. On no account give it a clout, as if it has any sense, it won't come to you next time.

As the dog learns to go round the sheep, give it a Slow Down whistle. Mine is a soft two-syllable whistle. I want the dog to continue on its feet, but at a slower pace.

This matter of working on its feet is a comparatively new phenomenon. There have been great ones in the past, such as John Holliday's Moss in the 1960s, but they were exceptional enough to be noteworthy. At the time there were too many 'clapping' or 'strong-eyed' dogs that would lie down and stare at the sheep for minutes at a time. They were time wasters in practical working situations, and tended to give trials a bad name.

Every dog requires a different approach. One thing can be applied to them all - commonsense. If you feel a training session has got nowhere, put the dog away on good terms, and sleep on the problem. There is no point whatsoever in persevering with a difficult session till the dog becomes bored stiff.

I have one dog at the moment that showed no great interest in sheep, although it is fourteen months old, and has been to see sheep every day for weeks. When it first saw sheep, it ran back to me. Then one day I saw its chin drop down and its ears go up. It set itself on seeing the sheep, and I knew that I had won.

### Using the Field or Pen

You must try to hold the sheep in mid-field, and away from the sides and corners. If you have a steady older dog to hold your little trainee flock into the centre, by all means use it. Your object is to manoeuvre the sheep so you are at 12 o'clock and the dog at 6 o'clock, directly opposite you. The dog is trailing its long line, so if things get out of hand you can step on the lead and haul the dog in.

### Style of Work

Most of my dogs work on their feet. This I feel gives them a great advantage. The sheep seem to give in more quickly. They can see the dog the whole time, whereas with a 'clapping' dog they may peep about and wonder what has happened to it when it lies flat.

Sid works on his feet, and was runner-up in the World Championship 2002. In his first season he won sixteen Nurseries and in the 2003 season won six Open Trials in six weeks.

Sid's son Dan works on his feet. He began working at six months, and is very, very quick on the uptake; he never needs telling anything twice. I've to be quite sure that what I've told him is the correct thing. for otherwise he might start doing something wrong, and be difficult to cure!

Both Sid and Dan are fairly tall dogs. This is an advantage when working in long grass, particularly in the moorland herbage known as 'blowgrass' on the Pennines. A small dog is

at a disadvantage in such conditions, which is not to decry small ones. There have been some wonderful examples among them, such as Tim Longton's little Nell.

I first saw Sid in a big trial in the Isle of Man. It had a 400 yards outrun, and this big good-looking, bare skinned dog did marvellously well. He was only thirteen months old at the time, and I managed to buy him at what then seemed a good price.

Some dogs have a knack of flipping a sheep over, but this is only for more experienced handlers. This started after I had had two new hips. Sid saw me struggling and decided to help me. He grabbed the sheep's far side fore leg and pulled it over. This can be very useful, but has its dangers: Sid was twice having trouble with sheep on the trials field, and grabbed a far leg. He was of course immediately disqualified, so I have had to teach him it must only be done on command. Once when we were shearing, Sid tipped over a sheep some yards away, and lay with his head across it. The shearer was amazed. When I walked up to the dog, I found that the ewe had hooked a horn under Sid's collar, which was why he didn't move! I released him, but said nothing to the shearer!

Sid, a tall dog!

Here are some of the most important things I learned from Jim.

We seldom refer to past breeding and pedigrees when buying pups. Some handlers are religious in keeping to certain lines, which is fine for them. However, over the years Jim has acquired a dog by what he sees it doing. I have seen him buy a dog and only then ask about the breeding. In the early days, because of my ignorance, I thought it funny listening to people talk about the parents of a pup. Parents, grandparents and even great grandparents in fact. I picked my first dog, Bob, because I liked his eyes!! Instantly he accepted me and vice versa.

I have, of course, with all the dogs been lucky to have possibly the best trainer in the world watching my every move. Jim has a very keen eye for a good dog and, if something has gone wrong on a run, he will know why. He is expert at spotting faults in a dog or handler. Some of those he tries to help will listen and some won't! Jim's favourite saying is "The boy wouldn't learn because the boy wouldn't listen". A sheepdog handler can only improve through constructive criticism. This is how I have learnt and still do.

When first training a young dog therefore, listen to the comments of others as they may see something you do not. This can make all the difference between an below average dog and a good one.

During the months of training Bob, I couldn't believe the progress we were making. Jim was busy with the pub but every day he explained some more to me about training a young dog. Never let your dog get away with one inch. When you give a command such as a stop it must be obeyed instantly. the trainable young dog should instinctively go round sheep at your feet. At the point of balance, stop them. This is often how the stop is taught. Only when the dog knows and obeys his stop command can further training progress.

There are three golden rules Jim has taught me concerning early training.
• 1 Never let your dog cross on its first early and small outruns.
• 2 Stop means stop.
• 3 Teach the young dog to stop at various points on the clockface, all followed by a few "walk on" commands.

During the early years I went to many trials and realised that Jimmy was different from many of the handlers there. Some had panic in their voices when things went wrong. Jimmy didn't.

When things were not right, his commands were more authoritative making the dogs listen. A panic command will cause the dog to panic. I knew then that he could somehow get inside a dog's head. That is why he is known as "The Dog Man".

Shirley is also a skilled artist, as this sketch shows. See also the One Man and His Dog chapter.

# Sheep Breeds

Jim with four different local breeds of sheep: Derbyshire Gritstones, Cheviots, Lonks and Whitefaced Woodlands.

The different breeds of sheep all have their own characteristics. They can of course vary within breeds, which may relate partly to the farms where they are kept. Some might be used to small well-fenced fields, others to wide open spaces. Some may have been well dogged, others treated roughly. Some Blackfaces reared on a rocky Scottish peninsula had never seen a retaining fence, and could jump any stone wall unless topped with barbed wire.

For a trial, it is far better if all sheep come from the same farm and have been handled in the same way. It necessitates a large flock, and is by no means easy to achieve.

George Hutton of Threlkeld, English Lake District, provides sheep for major trials within range. George is a keen Swaledale breeder, shepherds his own sheep, and knows them very well. He has a flock large enough to allow scope for selection, so draws off any that are lame, weak, or particularly stubborn or flighty. The result is that every runner is faced with as near identical a packet as anyone could have hoped.

Today's dogs must be adaptable. In addition to varying types of weather, from hot sun to driving rain and strong winds, they may have to face carnivals, crowds, gunfire and parachutists. On a city course, there will inevitably be someone exercising a dog with a limited idea of control. Today's Border Collie must learn to cope with such matters in a manner unthought of a generation ago.

Which is the best breed of sheep for trialling? It's an idle question, for you must make do with whatever is turned out of the release pen. The late Oliver Wall, a keen triallist from Weardale, County Durham, favoured Welsh Mountains, and these little sheep trotted before him steadily enough to gain a place in the English National team. For this type of sheep a dog must adapt its style, and keep well back. It's the same at the pen; these little shy and active animals must be given plenty of time. Push them too hard, and they will scatter. I believe in helping a dog as much as possible at the pen, and this applies particularly to flighty types.

Big Suffolk and Texel crosses react quite differently. The dog must keep them moving on, and not give in to them. They must look enormous to a dog, who has only its 'eye' and will power to move them, as it knows it must not grip.

Swaledales are not too bad, nor are Blackfaces. They are of course commonly found in Scotland, along with that other native breed, the Hill Cheviot. This smart, white-faced, white-woolled sheep is very sharp, always looking for an escape route. Other dark-faced, horned hill breeds such as Lonk and Derbyshire Gritstone are similar to Swaledales. The Woodland Whiteface has slightly different characteristics, possibly because of the merino blood believed to have been introduced in the reign of King George III. It is always used at the Harden Moss trials on the South Pennines.

In the USA they may run 'hair' sheep, very active and with no coats to hinder them. I have seen a flock of 30 of these sharp sheep being used all day at one trial, and they seemed as active at night as when they started. Hair sheep are very clever in finding out a dog's weaknesses. Much the same may be said of Hebridean, a primitive breed from the Islands but popular with mainland handlers as they keep moving all the time. When training a pup, it is a great asset if it can begin its career with sheep that move freely in front of it. 'Strong' sheep that stand and look at you are frustrating for the trainee (and for anyone else).

On Yorkshire's east coast there are some big, powerful sheep used to fold on turnip fields on the Yorkshire Wolds. The winter wind there blows straight in from the Arctic, and only strong, heavy-fleeced sheep could survive. They are liable to put their heads down and look at a dog, which brings me back to the Border Collie's adaptability.

# Doubling

At the filming of the 1987 One Man and His Dog: Phil Drabble talks with brace competitors John Paterson for Scotland with Don and Jix, and Jim for England with Cap I (Fonzi) and Cap II.

'Brace' or 'doubles' is the term for running two dogs together. At trials level it is less popular than formerly; I note that not all the 2004 Scottish National brace places were filled. Smaller trials do not usually have doubles classes, but the bigger, well established trials like Harden Moss, Royal Lancashire and Bamford do.

It's nice to work doubles. I was lucky, as I happened to own some good brace dogs early in my career. Fleet and Clyde won the International at Bala in 1973, and Bonnie and Clyde were a successful and well known pair. Here at Deerplay an extensive 150 acres pasture is gathered by sending one dog up either side, enabling the ground to be covered completely, easily and with no fuss.

To start doubling, you need two well trained collies. They should have a season's trialling behind them. In fact, doubles helps put the finer points on dogs usually run in singles, as their obedience must be instantaneous and complete.

Your doubles pair must be well balanced. It is no use having one that is always dashing in, and another that hangs back. Ideally, both should be on different whistles. Some handlers speak the dog's name before giving the command, but I don't find that as satisfactory.

I start to train a doubles pair on a small area, with a small bunch of sheep. I keep one dog lying by my side, and practice penning with the other. For that you need to erect a normal size pen perhaps eight feet by four feet, into which the 'active' dog works its sheep while the other is immobile. The dog that has done the penning should then lie at the pen mouth for a few minutes, to ensure that the sheep stay in. On no account should the other one get carried away and start to help. Then swop them round, so that the spectator becomes the worker. Patience and firmness are obviously called for, but you must have this stage foolproof before proceeding. Always remember that things happen at a trial that do not happen at home, and that dogs often respond to the trials atmosphere by becoming over-excited.

The stop whistle is the same for both dogs – one long sharp blast. Then you call the dog's name when you want it to proceed, and its appropriate movement command. This is where the value of separate whistles comes in. These are so difficult to describe on paper that the reader will be better served talking to experienced handlers about the range of simple commands.

On entering your first brace trial, you must be able to assess the speed of both dogs. The aim is for them to arrive behind the sheep together. At one time the dogs were not allowed to cross once behind the sheep, but it is often better practical shepherding if they do, and judges nowadays do not penalise the move. Once they have crossed at the top of the field, they must then keep to their respective sides, and are heavily penalised if they do not.

Again, do not forget that trials dogs tend to move up a gear, so it is vital that you stay mentally on your toes and try to anticipate the next moves.

You have now completed the outrun, with both dogs behind the sheep. Then comes the lift, and to make a successful lift with two dogs is quite a feat in itself. Both dogs should lift simultaneously. If the timing is not right, one lands too early and may lift the sheep before the other arrives. That of course loses points. You must know your dogs, which you will if you have reached the doubling stage. One course may be longer than the other eg: the dog on your right may have further to run than the one on your left. It might be quicker or slower, or perhaps less inclined to stop when reaching its sheep from the outrun. All these factors must be balanced.

Here is an example of what happened when I ran Fleet and Clyde in the brace. If Fleet got to his sheep first, he would wait. If Clyde arrived first, he was so pushy that he would take the sheep on his own. Therefore I had to time the two runs so that Fleet had steadied himself before his partner arrived to try to take over.

After that, the next stages are easier. The fetch gets underway with a dog on either side, and here the wisdom of your choice in working a balanced pair is tested.

The sheep are heading for the shepherd, and should pass him in a tight turn. That means that the outside dog has to make more ground than its partner. I am sometimes asked if the dogs always work on one particular side, but the answer is no. I like tham to be adaptable, but some may do differently.

You are now proceeding along the triangular drive with a dog on either side. As in the singles, staight lines are the rule, swinging onto the cross drive and then turning for home, and retaining that straight line.

In the shedding ring, things are different from the singles trial. There are usually six, eight or ten sheep, which must be split into two equal lots. To do this, use one dog, leaving the other lying down. I have the sheep in front of me, the working dog beyond them, and the other one of the partnership behind me and outside the ring.

You should not have to worry about the spare dog. If it moves or tries to join in, you have not done your work at home properly. Sometimes there will be a buzz from the crowd which usually means that the second dog is trying to join in. It plays its part once the shed is complete, as the sheep are alllowed out of the ring, to be guarded by the second dog and not allowed to retreat out of sight.

On completing the shed, the next stage is penning. The first pen has no gate, and after a successful pen the dog is made to lie down at the pen mouth, keeping the sheep in. Then the second dog takes over, and brings the split-off sheep to the mouth of the second pen, which has a gate this time. It pens them to a huge sigh of relief from the handler as he slams the gate home.

This reaction is the more heartfelt as a mistake in the doubles can result in a real wreck, far worse than anything in the singles. Your brain has been working overtime, and only absolute concentration has seen you through.

I remember trying to pen at the Bala International, and was having difficulty with the second lot of sheep. That circle seemed the loneliest place on earth. You could hear a pin drop, and a voice from the crowd floated over: 'He's only got two minutes left!' Fortunately I managed to pen very shortly after that, to win the trial.

# Great Dogs & Great Men

Tot Longton and his son Thomas with their International winning dogs Jess (Aberystwyth, 1983) and Bess (Beaumaris, 1986)

There's a long tradition behind sheepdog handling, and to be successful needs a lot of sheep work, a lot of study and a knowledge of how to handle sheep. The full-time shepherd has of course a big advantage. Not only is he constantly in practice, but his daily work includes running his dogs over long distances. I ran a number of different Nursery dogs each year, and this undoubtedly helped. Yet no one gets to the top in any sphere without considerable help from others. I have been exceptionally lucky in being brought up in an area containing a lot of 'dog men'. Away from the main sheep areas, sheep dog enthusiasts have less stimulation and fewer opportunities. It is all the more credit to them when they overcome such drawbacks.

Tot Longton must always remain at the top of my list of helpers. He was christened Thomas, but Tot was his invariable name. I was young and keen, and he gave me more encouragement than anyone else.

In the early 1960s, Tot would ring up and announce a trial the following Saturday. Would I like to go? Of course I would, but told him that I hadn't entered. 'That's all right; I've entered for you' he would say.

This set up a friendship destined to last until Tot's death. Some handlers were polite and showed an interest when I approached them, but seemed to be holding something back. Tot gave me the full amount of his knowledge and experience, no matter how often I pounded him with questions. I watched his runs with the greatest interest, learning something from every one.

Sometimes his brother, Tim, would come along. I think they enjoyed the jokes I told, as I was quite a lad about town then, and passed on the stories circulated by my workmates.

Tim and Tot took me to places I'd never been to before. We went down to Worcestershire, to Llyr Evans country. Who that witnessed it could ever forget Llyr and his great dog Coon, run mainly on voice commands? Llyr calling , 'Coon, Coon,' across the trials fields comes back to me down the years.

We travelled to Wales, to Pershore and the Vale of Evesham, to Cumbria and the Scottish Borders. Tot liked me to do some of the driving, which I enjoyed, and this was a small means of repaying. I would sometimes set off at 3 am, to drive to Lee End, Quernmore, near Lancaster, where he farmed. He might have milked the cows before I arrived or, if it was a really early start, his wife and the young Thomas would have milked for him.

We made these trips regularly for some years, doing two trials in one day. Nearer home on the northern circuit we did four or five. We would arrive, give our names to the secretary, run our dogs, and depart for the next venue. En route we would of course dissect the runs we had just made. I have fond memories of one particular circuit that we covered regularly. The first trial was at Brinskill, near Bolton, followed by Shap on the A6 overlooking the Lakeland fells. From there we travelled to West Ward, Cumbria, where we ran our dogs before setting off to Alston, that high market town in the mid-Pennines where it can snow in almost any month except perhaps July and August. Our final stint took us to an evening trial at Winton, Kirkby Stephen, Cumbria. Between us we returned with a capful of prizes.

One day I won at Brinskill and again at Shap, where I had a clean sheet – no deductions. Tot won at West Ward, we were both high in the placings at Alston, and I won Winton at night.

Tot had a genius for working wild sheep. I used to marvel at the way he got those really touchy sheep into the pen. No matter how they tried to scatter, Tot always seemed to have a dog that could settle them. It was a natural gift that he couldn't describe, any more than I could apply the same techniques and be successful. One of his tricks was to 'blare' softly at the approaching sheep in a way that a shepherd does in the field or on the fell when he is wanting the sheep to follow him. Others must have done the same, but it always seemed to work with Tot. I watched and studied, but never quite brought it off with flighty sheep in the way that Tot could. He was a real artist at his job.

He enjoyed his trialling, and life in general. He wore the same broad smile when coming off with a trainee dog that had made a mess of things as he did when winning the sheep dog world's very top honours, which he did on several occasions.

There was nothing hidden. He was judging once – he judged as the occasion demanded, though he preferred running - when a passing competitor said: 'Don't judge my dog; I'm just running it for running's sake'. Tot replied: 'I'm here to judge, and if you run your dog, I shall judge it along with the rest.'

Tot Longton won the International in 1983 with his bitch Jess.

He and I were running on the final day of the Cardiff International in 1971. It was a very big course, with a left hand outrun. Tot had a beautiful run with Gyp, who gathered her first lot of sheep – it is always a double gather at the International - and went off for the second lot in fine style. She brought them all together into the shedding ring. Then calamity struck. None of the sheep had ribbons on them, so the Shed could not proceed. There was nothing for it but to run again later in the day.

The day developed into a scorcher. We realised that Tot's little bitch was overheated, but fortunately I had noticed a hose pipe halfway along the ground. We took Gyp there, and cooled her down by running the hose pipe over her for a quarter of an hour. She completed her course for the second time, and Tot often spoke of the occasion, and how lucky it was that I had spotted that hose pipe.

I was fourth in that trial, which Jock Murray won. I brought my first lot of sheep just nicely, but crossed in front of the second lot. Tot said I didn't give my dog enough time to see his second lot of sheep, and he was right. I had turned Clyde too quickly, and possibly lost the trial through undue haste at a vital point.

In the course of these journeys through some of Britain's finest hill country I met a great many more successful handlers, and learnt something from all of them. Mike Perrings, who sadly died just before his term of office with the International Sheep Dog Society, used to say that the best thing about sheep dog trialling was the comradeship among fellow competitors and how right he was.

Alan Jones with Roy were a really famous pair. At the beginning of my trialling career I remember seeing Alan run doubles in Scotland with Roy and Glen. Alan was a terrific handler and Roy was one in a million. A black, white and tan prick eared dog, Roy had power, stamina and speed. He worked in a relaxed way and gave his sheep confidence. Alan talked a lot to his dogs rather than using a whistle and was a very assured handler. The pair went from strength to strength, gathering many prestigious awards along their way.

Raymond MacPherson and Zac, who won the Supreme Championship twice in 1975 and 1979, were an outstanding pair. Raymond is one of the best and most highly competitive handlers of our times and has represented England on many occasions.

Another impressive trialling duo were Bobby Dalziel and Wisp, another pair to triumph twice

Jim competing at Harden Moss

steep hill where he may go out of sight. On the lift, the dog has to cross drive slightly the wild Welsh sheep down the hillside and through the middle gate hole in the fence. Again a slight cross drive fetch is needed to bring the sheep towards a fence on the handler's right hand side. In a change of direction, the sheep are pushed uphill between a hurdle and the fence. There is another set of hurdles returning towards the handler culminating in the difficult task of penning. The top dogs from this event go through to the final. This trial has a history going back more than 100 years.

Jim and John Harvey at Harden Moss

Winners of the Isle of Man team event are David Broster, Alf Kyme, judge Raymond MacPherson, and Jim.

Overseas trips work the other way as well. Two Norwegian handlers, Henry Aliseike and three times Continental Champion Jaran Knive talk to Jim at the 2004 Bodfari North Wales Open trial

### Isle of Man Trial

Another annual trial with a large variety of different countries participating is the Isle of Man trial. There was double victory for me and my team (England) comprising D Broster, A Kyme and myself. The individual was won with Cap.

It is a National type course with a 400 yard outrun and shed, pen and single. Raymond MacPherson was judging that day and an early morning run by Gwyn Jones (Penmachno) set a high standard. This was a superb run with only two and a half points lost - it looked unbeatable. Alf and David had two decent runs and when my turn came I knew I had to go for the perfect run. Cap went out on a perfect outrun to the back of the sheep and picked them up. They came on straight as a die. I didn't see my dog until he got near my feet. Turning the sheep, Cap never broke his pace but kept them moving steadily away on a straight drive. He finished with superb shed, pen and single losing only one point in all.

Raymond later gave a speech and commented he had never seen a run like it. He said he had taken one point off but didn't know where from.

### Hebden Bridge.

There's an interesting and very old trial at Hebden Bridge, West Yorkshire. The dog goes straight from the handler to a river with a little bridge. The sheep are four hundred yards away at the start, within sight of dog and handler, but then the dog has to run two hundred yards downhill to the river, find the bridge and negotiate it, and be recast on the other bank.

Each dog must deal with these problems in its own way. Some dogs are going so fast that they miss the bridge, which initially puts them out of the running. Give a right-hand whistle once your dog has crossed the bridge, and it is then up to the dog to find the sheep up the hill, as they are out of sight of both dog and handler. They do a triangular course, culminating in a pen.

### Patterdale,

situated in the Lake District, is another annual trial that we enjoy attending. The field and trial are both different from any other. Set in a valley bottom, surrounded by the hills of the Lake District, this event is described as a dog show with a hound trail and terrier show. There is also an athletic cross country race.

The trial course is on a flat field where the sheep are picked up. The course then continues up on a hillside which is rocky and dotted with trees. Hurdles are set between rocks and trees. The dog returns with three sheep back onto the flat to pen.

A few competitors at Burnley Show in 1966.

placed quietly on the same spot for each run.

Many trials can be spoilt by the way in which

# Trials history

PRICE 2d.

## ☞ BALA ☜

## Sheep-Dog TRIALS,

. HELD ON .

### TUESDAY, OCTOBER 31st, 1899.

President,

R. J. LL. PRICE, ESQ., RHIWLAS, BALA.

Vice-President,

COL. BURTON, ERYL ARAN, BALA.

*Judges,*

MR. WILLIAM EVANS, BLAENYCOED, YSBYTY.

„ JOHN JONES, PENLAN, LLANGOLLEN.

*Chairman of Committee,*

DR. WILLIAMS, TAWELFAN, BALA.

*Hon. Treasurer,*

J. PARRY-EVANS, ESQ., N.P. BANK, BALA.

*Hon. Secretary,*

MR. H. E. PARRY, HIGH STREET, BALA.

WYTHNOS A'R ERYR Office, Bala.

## ☞ RULES. ☜

1. All Dogs entered to be on the ground—Open Stakes 9-30 a.m., Local Stakes 8 a.m., and except when working, must be held by a cord or chain, under penalty of disqualification.

2. No Dogs, except those competing, will be allowed on the ground.

3. Any Dog injures a Sheep will be disqualified, and the Owner of the Dog will be liable for the damage.

4. No one will be allowed with the Dog competing except the man working it, and he will be placed where the Committee directs.

5. The Committee, with the assistance of the Judges, will decide the time to be allowed to each Dog.

6. The Judges have the power of ordering up as soon as they please any Dog that commits a flagrant error, and their decision in all cases shall be final.

7. In case of insufficient merit, the Judges are empowered to withhold the prizes according to their discretion.

The cover and (below) the rules from the 1899 Bala sheepdog trial programme.

Mankind has always had a competitive spirit. Whose horse is the fastest? Whose team can plough a straight furrow? Whose dog can work sheep the best?

These questions have lifted the standard of countryside skills throughout Britain and from there to the rest of the world. They have resulted in better animals for a given purpose, and a class of handlers, male and female, who exploit them to the full. These facts have never been recognised by any Government since 1945, but they are very true.

The first dog show was held in Newcastle in 1859, but was based purely on appearance. Skills were untested, yet such events brought together breeders of working gun dogs, working sheep dogs, and dogs bred for appearance.

Thus when E S Shirley founded the kennel club in 1873, he persuaded his friend Richard John Lloyd Price, to organise a working test. Mr Lloyd Price was squire of Rhiwlas' 64,000 acres in North Wales, and it was on his land that the first sheepdog trials open to all comers were staged. Mr Lloyd Price's grandson, Lt Col Peter Price, presented the awards at the International Sheepdog Society Centenary trials. In 1980, the International again returned to Bala under the presidency of the founder's great-grandson, Mr Robin Price. On 6th July 1873, The Field magazine published a letter stating that the Welsh squire was to organise a 'novelty', with the help of the Rhiwlas Field Trials Committee - a gundog society. This 'novelty' was to be a sheepdog trial 'open to the world.' A trusty and experienced shepherd was to help with the judging, and the entry fee was to be 10 shillings, which was then a lot of money. The Field on 18th October that year reported that, in addition to their great historical interest, they reflected the sound thinking of the organisers and the necessity to test a working dog on its basic craft. The tests on two separate courses were for dogs to gather, drive, and pen over 500 to 800 yards respectively. It is noteworthy that these measurements approximate to the present International Sheepdog Society standards. The wild and unpredictable nature of the 'wiry little Welsh sheep', as mentioned in the report, has not changed that much either   Another   comment to the effect that the best way to master these sheep was to 'chase them round and tire them out first' would certainly be banned today, but reflects the frustration of generations of dog handlers. The modern equivalent is a wish for a 'Death Ray' for ewes that simply refuse to flock, understood by anyone who had competed in a trial.

A crowd of 300 watched the first trial, standing on a grassy mound. Eric Halsall revisited the scene over a century later, and described it in his splendid book 'Sheepdog Trials'. Relics of an old tribal battle have been found on the field, and the rock to which is now fixed a plaque commemorating the first sheepdog trial had been used in days gone by as a target for the lead bullets of the old militia. The idea of a plaque was encouraged by a visiting sheepman from New Zealand.

Bala had the basic ingredients, with no useless stunts. Prize money was, and still is, very small. It would be strange if there was no betting in an age when our forebears seemed to wager on all sorts of animal feats, but betting has always been banned under International Sheep Dog Society rules.   Those first Bala trials stimulated interest. There followed others. The Scottish Borders were a hotbed of the sport. It is where the 'Border' part of the name originated. Farms were large, and each employed a number of full-time working shepherds. Each spent his days almost solely on sheep work, 'raking' the flock to the heights each evening away from the midges, and bringing them down in the morning. Thus the ground was evenly grazed, and over-grazed pockets of worm infection avoided. Naturally every man thought his dog the best in the valley, but the only way to prove it was through the sheepdog trial.

The first Border trials were staged at Byrness in the Rede valley, Northumberland. This was a good hill test, dogs having to cross the fair-sized River Rede and run half a mile to their sheep on the opposite bank. Two months previously it is said the Welsh shepherds challenged the Scots, having lost first place at Bala.

The entire Bala show was to be transferred to Alexandra Park, London. This proved a disaster as the little Welsh wether lambs proved too much for the collies, and disappeared, or were sold by auction at the end.   Queen Victoria was always interested in dogs, and was said to have had a special exhibition trial run for her benefit.

Carnworth Agricultural Society staged the first trials in Scotland in the early 1870s. This was on the fringe of the Pentland Hills in Lanark. In 1870, Lord Arthur Cecil of Orchardmains, Innerleithen, paid £10 for the winning bitch at West Linton, then a lot of money. At Jedforest in 1882 there were 12 entries, with the winner described as a gentle black and white bitch, of great polish. Her owner was Tom Turnbull of Attonburn, a sound Eastern Borders farm whose Hill or Southcountry Cheviot sheep figure in the earliest flock books. New Cumnock staged a trial with £6 first prize money in 1897. The winner was the 18 month old Lock, handled by John Hastings of Glenwhargen. This collie became the first to win two premium trial honours by repeating its success in 1898. In 1899 this hillside course with its 600 yards gather attracted 500 spectators and 32 dogs. The next year the course was snow-covered, with 31 entries.

In 1900, Alex Millar greeted the new century by winning the New Cumnock event with the five-year-old black and tan Bruce. He was then a young man, but became a consistent winner, as he won three International Farmers, three International Brace, and nine Scottish National titles.

Alex - or 'Sandy' - Millar believed that you have got to make a friend of your dog. 'I talk a great deal to my dogs, try to make them feel that we're partners and pals, and there is very little I say that they don't understand.' He believed that a good dog was born, not made.

A watershed occurred at the Hawick trials in 1873. William Wallace of Otterburn worked his dog with a mere hiss at hand, and with a low whistle at a distance. This was a major break from the usual noisy, arm-waving style of shepherding then practised, and pioneered the minimum commands and quiet control expected today. Dogs at Bala in 1873 were reported as yelping and barking, and voice was liberally used in efforts to control them. On some farms this still applies, witness the hilarious Henry Brewis cartoons, depicting an untidy-looking farmer with a stick, dancing up and down, and waving his stick in the air to a series of expletives.

William Wallace won the second championship

organised by the International Sheep Dog Society in 1907 with Moss. Years later he was to repeat this feat wih Meg at the 1922 International Championship at Criccieth.

James Scott, of Troneyhill, Ancrum, near Jedburgh in Teviotdale, was also a quiet and efficient handler. He believed that trials played a big part in improving shepherding skills, and regretted that farmers were lukewarm to the importance and value of a well-trained collie.

The International Sheep Dog Society was formed in 1906 by a dozen or so sheep men at Haddington, East Lothian. This was really a regional meeting, but it grew in stature as if to implement its ambitious, all-embracing title. The purpose of the meeting was to sort out basic arrangements and methods of testing a dog. Those present were also concerned to interest the public in the shepherd, and to bring shepherds together for their mutual benefit. Few societies can have so completely fulfilled their early, tentative steps. Membership never exceeded one hundred in the years before World War One cast its dark shadow over the established order.

The first post-War trial in 1919 was under the secretaryship of James Reid, an Airdrie solicitor whose reign lasted until beyond World War Two. And reign it certainly was. James Reid shaped and steered the Society into its present form, and created a championship course that fully tested every one of the collie's shepherding duties. All today's worthwhile trials are based on this original concept.

One of the judges at the 1921 event at Ayr was Welshman E Jones Jarrett, who brought Wales into the international scene. The following September the International Trials were held at Criccieth in Wales, and the staging of National trials to select teams for the International was started. To this day, any dog competing in the International has won its 'cap' on merit.

In 1927 the first team contest was held, for a trophy for the country with the best overall standard of shepherding. In 1929 the first Brace or Doubles contest was held, followed in 1937 by the popular and impressive Driving Championship over the length of the course.

Irish sheep men competed with a team of three single dogs at Ayr in 1961, to be joined by Eire in 1965, with collies from the Isle of Man included in the Irish section. To return to the dogs, the 1923 champion was George Brown's Spot. After this victory he was exported to America, and became the foundation sire of the North

Ashton Priestley competing at a Lakeland trial

American Sheepdog Society's Stud Book.

In 1928, Jim Wilson won the first of his nine Supreme titles when aged 27. A sheep farmer at Holmshaw, Moffat, Dumfriesshire, and later at Whitehope Farm at the head of Leithen Water above Innerleithen, Jim was a master breeder of both Blackface sheep and Border Collies. In 19 years of top level competitive trialling J M, as he was known to the sheepdog fraternity, won 55 National and International trophies.

The onset of World War Two in 1939 halted competitive trials, but not the need for good sheep workers. The nation needed its farmers to produce food for survival, and Border Collies played their full part. The top breeding lines were maintained, and this was to be proved when trials resumed after 1945. Jim Wilson's Glen headed the International at Worcester in 1948, having won the Scottish National in 1946. From then till 1950, sheep dog people rejoiced in the easier times and more available fuel. It was a rosy period for sheep dog trials and for all agricultural shows. Country people wanted to move around once more, and renew friendships. David Daniel's Chip worked daily by herding Welsh ewes on the Black Mountains, and won for Wales that country's fourth Supreme honour at Ayr in 1949. He did so again in 1952.

Ashton Priestley from the Derbyshire Peak District won the Supreme for England in 1951. Familiar winning names of that epoch included Bob Fraser's Mindrum strain, and Tot Longton's prick-eared Mossie.The Hyde Park trials under Daily Express sponsorship helped bridge the gap between town and country, and are still spoken of with affection by participants. Thomson McKnight's Gael became only the second bitch in 29 years to take the Supreme. Tim Longton won the 1966 International with Ken. That makes a neat point at which to end this early resume, for I was then actively involved in the trials scene.

# Overseas Trips

Even Jim can still learn new tricks! Here he is in Norway with Allan the sheep shearer, whose dog had an unusual but effective method of catching a rogue sheep.

Jim at a clinic in America with Roger Deschambeault.

### AMERICAN TRIPS

I have enjoyed trips to America and Canada for over 20 years. Hospitality in these two countries is most generous. They have imported all the best bloodlines of Border Collies from all the corners of Britain and Ireland. They now have a well established gene pool and fewer dogs are being imported.

On first visiting these countries I found that, although they were keen to learn, they needed more help in their training. A lack of sheep sense was hampering them. This can only be learnt through experience of handling sheep. A few of the handlers dogged sheep around a course, then asked for a re-run, not knowing the fault for the poor run lay with them.

As the years went on, there was a vast improvement in dogs and handlers, who managed the sheep and trials much more easily. This was largely due to good handlers from Britain giving lessons and clinics. The improvement has culminated in 37 dogs hoping to come to the World Trial in 2005 from USA and 9 from Canada.

An outstanding veteran sheepdog handler was

Ralph Pulfer (sadly recently deceased). He was possibly self taught and a cattle man who could manage most dogs sold to him. Years ago we took him a dog called Clint and, in a very short time, he was winning trials with this dog. Ralph passed on his knowledge and training methods throughout America and Canada. Twelve years ago we travelled with Ralph and his wife, Lenor, in their pick up twin cab, towing a huge mobile home. We drove for 12 hours, from Doug Peterson's in Iowa to Kathy and Larry Connors in Missouri. Usually we arrived a day or two before the trial started. Watching competitors arrive is splendid. Huge pick ups tow enormous mobile homes and people travel thousands of miles to participate in a trial.

These two countries have now become quite self contained within the sheepdog world, having imported top dogs for 30 years and more and advanced their handling skills. Scottish international handlers are now resident in these countries including Jack Knox, Tommy Wilson and Alastair MacRae. These men and others have all done wonders for the sheepdog folk in the USA.

Alastair MacRae and family. We visited them when judging in the USA.

Jim in Norway.

## NORWAY

After completing several trips abroad, we were invited to go to Norway. This was a very interesting fortnight, seeing different ways of farming and different ways of training dogs. The country was very, very heavily wooded, and nearly every sheep wore a bell. Herding was done by listening to the tinkling of the bells, all of which seemed to be identical.

When gathering, the dogs' ears would go up, and they would set off in the direction of the bells. The shepherd could hear the jingle, but could do nothing until the sheep appeared from that very thick undergrowth. The dogs were Border Collies bred on English and Scottish lines, and great care had been taken in their selection. The clinics were very enjoyable.

Commands in Norwegian are: Benstra for Left, Hiera for Right; and Dick for Stop. It took me a full week to learn my Right and Left, so imagine how long it takes a young dog.

Most of the sheep were of an old-fashioned type that went back to the Vikings. They were horned, with self-shedding coarse hair, and were about the size of a Swaledale. The other breed was white-faced. like a Cheviot cross, and very wild. They were very skilled jumpers, and could clear a fence of pig net set on a bank, but they responded to a dog.

For our first clinic, several people brought their own dogs, mostly young ones, and pretty good to train once they had found out who was boss. Then we had two spare days in which our wonderful host took us out to sea in a rowing boat. We caught our own fish, including three mackerel on one hook, and cooked them in a log cabin. This was a new experience for us as hill people.

Handlers at the next clinic we took were slightly more experienced. We were trying to shed off six dark from six light sheep, with the rest 50 yards away. I tried to shed off the white sheep, but a black one returned to the main group. A sheep shearer called Allan brought it back, his dog zigzagging as it kept its eye on that one sheep. I had never seen a dog do ths before.

The Norwegians have their own Stud Book, and are very, very keen to learn. They were interested in everything I said, but this had to be through one lad who could interpret, as few could speak English.

One dog at that clinic was so hard that he would definitely have killed a sheep if he got to them; he was a real tiger of a dog. The dog was worked for half an hour till his tongue was hanging out. I took a short whip, and he came at me as if he would kill me. He would certainly have had hold of me. I hit him across the snout, and after that I trained him every day. After four days the dog got round the course, the battle was over, his owner was over the moon, and thought I was God.

I then judged one Open and One Novice trial, with 50 and 30 dogs at each. Shirley was time keeping and booking. We made many friends, saw some wonderful mountains and fjords, and returned home.

### ITALY

Travelling to this beautiful country is always a pleasure. We stayed quite high up in the mountains, a three or four hour drive from Rome. Our invite came from a group of five people who were watching the World Trial in Bala in 2002. They were so impressed with the way Sid ran in the final and mainly how he took his "Look Back" command. This is what they wanted to learn to do with their dogs. Already they could handle a dog at National level. However, their jobs were those of plumber, male hairdresser,

student, butcher and shop assistant. The student was the interpreter. Our accommodation was an apartment in an old converted farm high on a hill, surrounded by fields of fruit trees. Lower down the hillside was a large flat field, where a National size course was erected. A Kelpie was brought onto the field and had a fair outrun, lift and fetch but it was difficult to get it to drive. The Border Collies all soon learnt to shed and "Look Back". At the end of the few days the sheepdogs were at a higher standard and able to run a National course. Our journey ended with two lovely days in Rome.

# One Man and His Dog

Jim in the commentary box alongside Gus Dermody for the Christmas 2004 edition.

One of Jim's carvings for the 2004 series.

September 1987; the prize giving for the One Man and His Dog doubles. Jim won with Cap I and Cap II.

After his success, Jim talks with Phil Drabble

*Jim competed in 'One Man and His Dog' in September 1987 at Derwent Water in the Lake District. The progamme was shown in 1988*

This picture with Cap II was used by the BBC to publicise the programme under the title 'Jimbo'

## Jim's One Man and His Dog

In 1987, England, Ireland, Scotland and Wales each had three singles runs and a doubles run. Situated on a lake side, the course was smaller than a National with a single and a pen at the end. Phil Drabble was the interviewer and Eric Halsall the commentator.

Having recently won the English National with Cap II at Seahouses, I was invited by the BBC to run him in the singles cometition. He paired with Cap I (Fonzi) in the doubles. The filming took place over three days. Cap II failed to qualify for the final competition, but he redeemed himself by taking the doubles with Fonzi. At this time, the programme went on for several weeks, allowing the public an insight into the farming community which created a lot of interest. Millions would watch the programme in 1987, with consequent benefit to the BBC.

It was an honour and a nice surprise to be asked last year (2004) to do some commentating on the show with Gus Dermody. It was very interesting to see how much hard work goes into making the programme. Everybody works well together behind the scenes. The hard work paid off this year because the viewing figures were up. If they get as high as they did in 1987 then maybe we will get the programme back as it was then.

It is still a brilliant programme to watch - enhancing all the qualities a Border Collie possesses at work with his master.

---

## Shirley's One Man and His Dog

In the year 2000, I won my first open trial with Bob. I was now running him consistently but our main struggle was at the pen. This was obviously due to lack of experience and lack of sheep sense. 2001, the foot and mouth year, we stopped going to trials all summer. The nursery trials started in October of that year with great care and attention to disinfection and sheep movement.

Following that Nnursery season, I gained a couple more wins with Bob in the open trials which earned us enough points to apply for a placing in the English National. I had watched many Nationals and never thought I would make the grade. However, I did and my first National with Bob was in 2002 at Bicester near Oxford. I had a good start and a bad finish. Sad to say, nerves got the better of me and I missed my second drive gates and failed to pen! After that day I vowed never to get that nervous again because I was only letting my dog down.

Then came the next shock - a telephone call from Gus Dermody inviting me to run Bob on "One Man and His Dog". I just couldn't believe it - 4 years previously I was perming ladies' hair and waxing legs!! I realised now that I had to put my best foot forward and listen to everything Jimmy could advise me on. If he saw me doing anything wrong he would roar like a lion. The same applies today!

Jimmy came with me to Longleat Estate in Bath, where they filmed the 2002 programme. It was a glorious week, but not too hot for the dogs. We met all the production team led by Daniel Brittain-Catlin. They were surprised, on meeting me, as I didn't look or act as if I lived on a farm!

The event again included teams for the four nations and most of the contenders I was meeting for the first time such as Frank Cashen and Glyn Jones (Selatyn). Some were International men.

Jimmy is my trainer and coach. He watches every trial we go to and works out all the difficult parts. This trial was no exception - he warned me about the first drive hurdle which was surrounded by small trees. In the gentle breeze the trees rustled so preventing the sheep from going straight through the drive hurdles. He warned me to keep the pressure up on the left hand flank.

The camera was rolling and it was my turn. Bob had a perfect outrun and a good gentle lift. We got our fetch gates and had a good turn at my feet. The drive began well and we kept a straight line to the drive hurdles but the wind got up a little and the sheep were slightly affected. Jimmys' words had flown out of my head. I let the pressure go on the left hand side and we missed the first drive gates. As soon as this happened I remembered Jimmy's words. However, I now gathered my thoughts and we continued to have a good run, getting the cross drive gates. Straight through the Maltese Cross and into the pen. I was so relieved. Many before and after me struggled to pen. Our run gained us enough points to win. Bob has been such a good dog for me and has many natural qualities. Jimmy was so happy and proud that day. He has trained and helped many of his friends to run dogs but I think I was his most difficult pupil!

Shirley alongside Clarissa Dickson-Wright at the filming of the 2002 edition with Ben Fogle behind them.

Shirley with Ben Fogle at the 2004 filming.

# Carving

As shown above, Jim made some stone carvings for the 2004 series of One Man and His Dog. How does he come to be such an accomplished artist?

"Even as quite a small boy I was always able to draw horses and dogs. I spent many happy hours doodling away, mainly on these two subjects.

About ten years ago I carved a dog out of soapstone. There are quarries and stone masons locally, so I was able to buy a suitable piece quite easily. A one-off piece from a stone mason is neither difficult nor expensive to acquire.

I equipped myself with the basic tools. With a hammer and chisel, carving from soft sandstone became a real possibility. I stick to things I know, mainly sheep dogs and sheep. I have not yet attempted a horse! Here are some pencil drawings. I have also worked in oils and pastels. It just shows that fine neat fingers are not necessary for competent art work. My hands are large and roughened by hard labour in the mines and, latterly, by outdoor work in all weathers. Sheep clipping is a good way of softening the hands, as the lanolin makes them very pliable.

My father was an artist in oils and my brother, Stanley, was a professional artist and a good one at that, so it must be in the family."

Above and opposite: sketches by Jim

Brian Irving's sketch of Jim with Fleet and Clyde

# At the End

A dog's lifespan is much shorter than a human's. It entails partings along the way. Every handler and stocksperson has to face this unpleasant fact. We all have our different ways of coping with the loss of our favourites.  Fleet was only ten years old when he died. He developed a form of kidney complaint, and took to drinking lots of water. The vet said that any treatment would mean only a very temporary alleviation, but I hadn't the heart to have him put down. He wasn't suffering physically.  The worst part was when I had to go to the hill, passing his kennel with another dog at heel. Fleet would howl and howl all the time I was away. Yet I couldn't take him; he couldn't have walked as far as the moor gate, let alone do any work.

Clyde was working sheep around the pens on a warm day, when I thought he was staggering about a bit. I put some straw in a disused cottage. Whenever I looked in he picked up his head, but that was all. I left him quietly to see if he would pull round, but next morning he was dead.

My son saw me go to the hill with the other dogs, and knew how upset I would be. By the time I returned, he had dug a grave for Clyde, and put a stone and a little cross on it. There is some deep soil near the village war memorial which stands, plain to see, in one of our top fields. Several of our dogs are buried near it.

I seldom dig the graves myself. It is too much like losing a close friend. When you have travelled thousands of miles with a dog, and stood at that lonely post with a few sheep in the distance, and the crowd tensing, you form a very special bond. I may have made a name for the dog, but it has also made a name for me.  Cap was a little dog that came from nowhere to win the English National three times. I was short of a dog for one trial, and borrowed him to make up the number. I never left without him after he won the first trial. In the end he had a stroke, and started going round and round. It was a sad end.

Cap was a lovely little character. He trailed about with my daughter Linda, who nicknamed him Fonzi after an American cartoon character. He loved playing with children, retrieving sticks or footballs. The remarkable thing about Cap, on arriving at a trial, was his unfailing habit of hopping out of the transport and slipping round to the front of the vehicle. There he would sit and take in the run in progress. He would watch and watch where the sheep came from, how they progressed down the field, how much space there was. Then after concentrating intensely for three or four runs, he would disappear to find some children to play with. I didn't see him again till my name came over the tannoy, and I called his name, and there he was.

Cap lived to seventeen. His health began to deteriorate, and he would set off for a bunch of sheep, but couldn't make it. All very sad.  When I lived with Mum and Dad at Turn Hill Farm, Dean Village, three or four dogs were buried there, each with a stone to mark them.

One of my saddest losses was more recent. I had a young three year old dog that I thought a lot about. One day I crossed the road and sent him round a big enclosure to gather sheep there. Suddenly a thick mist dropped down; remember our house is at 1350 feet.

There was no sign of dog or sheep, and I made my way back home, expecting him to find his own way. Suddenly a car drew up, and the driver asked if I had lost a dog. I went as he directed, and found a crumpled smashed-up heap and bits of car body and number plate. There was no hope for the dog, who died within minutes. The car driver did not stop, but must have known what had happened.

Afterwards I regretted that I had not gone to seek him, but we can all be wise after the event. All good sheepdog people know this feeling, that they might have done differently to care for a certain dog, that they did not spot sickness in time, or they were too busy with other things. The most we can do is to enjoy and care for the dogs under our control while we have them. Sometimes when sitting in front of the fire on a winter's night, I think back over the good dogs I've had.

Often a leading triallist is associated in his fellows' minds with just one dog. Think of John Richardson, and Wiston Cap immediately springs to mind, though John had several other excellent dogs.

Tot Longton's Rob is another, as is Thomson McKnight's Gael, and Tim Longton's Ken.

Glyn Jones had that great dog Taff, while Llyr Evans and his vocal commands to Bosworth Coon are an abiding memory.

John Holliday's Moss, working on his feet when that trait was less common, comes to mind, while Pat and Coon were irretrievably linked with Eric Elliott on those Derbyshire Peak District hills, and running Brace on the trials field.

Readers will have their own favourites. I would have difficulty in placing just one of my dogs above the others. Would it be Fleet, who really launched my name both as a winner and as a stud dog, or Sid, runner-up in the 2003 World Trials, or some other name? I'm just thankful to have had so many great companions during my life.

Edward Hart writes: I had a red and white Border Collie named Brick, out of a favourite little red bitch, Rinn. Brick was developing into a very useful work dog. My sheep were pastured on a long, narrow, sideways-sloping field with a steep bank at one end, surmounted by a spinney full of blackthorn suckers. The sheep would retreat behind this little wood, and each day I would send Brick round to them to save me walking the full distance. He became adept at this simple manoeuvre. One day I sent him off as usual. However there was not the usual response of a little flock trotting along with Brick behind. I waited and whistled with growing impatience, but when I finally walked round, Brick was lying there dead of a heart attack. He was an apparently 100 per cent fit dog, still in early life. Kipling said; 'beware of giving your heart to a dog to tear', but my shepherding trips were never the same again.

Years before I mentioned the death of another farm collie to a city lady. 'You farmers don't feel these things like we do,' she said. 'You are so used to stock being sold or slaughtered that you get used to it.' How wrong she was. The dogs that accompany our daily work routine become part of us. When one dies, we remember its little tricks, jumping a fence always in a certain place, popping through a particular smout hole in a drystone wall or splashing across a stream at the most fordable point.

The countryman or woman may not say very much, but the feelings towards their working companion are very real. Another touching story of an old helpmate is told by Roy Dent, Shepherd of the Year 1976, in Edward Hart's book 'The Hill Shepherd' (David and Charles 1977). The scene was Glen Whelt, Weardale, Co Durham.

'When Moss was twelve years old, he was retired, and became fat, heavy and deaf. One morning as his shepherd was setting off with tractor and trailer, Moss came up, looked at him, and begged to be allowed to accompany him. Stopping near as large stretch of fell, the shepherd found a few ewes that needed driving away, and thought Moss would love to do his old job, so he set the dog behind them, a fifty yards drive being planned. Moss thought differently. Right round the boundary of 600 acres he went, and being deaf couldn't hear anything of his handler's shouts and whistles. Because of his weight the old dog could only paddle slowly round, and the shepherd's exasperation grew as time passed. Eventually Moss arrived with a large packet of ewes, and never did a dog look so happy, smiling and pleased with himself.'

# Jim's Trials Successes

At Burnley Nursery Trial, 1971/2 season: Richard Haggis, Eric Halsall, Stanley Dungworth, Danny Wild and Jim with Sweep, a son of Fleet.

Here is a list of Jim Cropper's trials successes, as compiled by the late Eric Halsall.

• 19 International 'caps' to 1990.
• 1964-65 Nursery season -
Rex - unregistered - won second prize on his first outing at Turn Hill Farm, Holme trials on 24th October, 1964. He had three placings in season - 2nd at Holme - 5th at Meltham - 3rd at Holme. Fleet started nursery trials at 18 months old in Oct 1966.
• 1966-67 season - finished with 23 awards, including 8 victories, in 31 trials.
• 1967 Fleet's first National 24.8.67 at Dovedale, not placed. Was second at Burnley in his first open season - 1967.
• 1967-68 - Nursery season - Cap (Cass) had 4 placings - including one win.
• 1968 - Fleet won Lowgill and Shap (with full points) and was English Driving Champion at the National at Darlington.
• 1968-69 Nursery season - Clyde won 16 placings including 8 victories.

• 1969 - Fleet won Burnley, Trawden, Lowgill, Littleborough, and at Royal Lancs. 7th in National trials - 8th in qualifying International - 5th in Supreme. Clyde won Caton. Fleet and Clyde won Bamford brace. Fleet and Bonnie won Royal Lancs brace. Bonnie and Clyde were reserve brace at English National.
• 1969-70 Nursery - Cap (sold to Alec Moore) had 12 awards. Tess had 3 awards including one victory.
• 1970 - Fleet won Alston, and English Driving Championships. Clyde won Nelson, Winton, Deerplay and had 22 awards in open competitions that year. Clyde was 5th in National at Manchester - 11th in International qualifying - 3rd in Supreme.
• Bonnie won Lowgill. Bonnie and Clyde won Royal Lancs and Pershore brace.
• 1970-71 Nursery - Vic won 21 awards including 4 victories.
• 1971 - Fleet won Nelson, Moorcock. 7th in National at Middlesborough. 19th in qualifying at International. Clyde won Brinscall, Todmorden, Royal Lancs. 12th in National - 9th in International

Jim won the Engish National Driving with Fleet at Darlington in 1969.

including one victory.
• 1974 - Fleet won Nelson, Winton. Clyde won Rydal - 9th in National at Leek - 15th qualifying International. Fleet and Clyde won brace at Dublin Spring Show in Ireland.
• 1974-75 Nursery - Don 3 awards - Cap 2 awards.
• 1975 - Clyde won Littleborough Cricket Field and Great Eccleston.
• 1975-76 Nursery - Nell one award - Patch 11 awards inc. 2 victories - Rob 10 awards inc. 1 victory.
• 1976 - Clyde won Nelson.
• 1976-77 Nursery - Jaff won 11 awards inc. 5 victories and Meltham Champ. Garry won 3 awards. Nap won 9 awards inc. 3 victories.
• 1977 - Clyde won Todmorden. Jaff won Lyme Park.
• 1977-78 - Nursery - Fan won 16 awards inc. 3 victories and Holme Champ. Ben won 13 awards inc. 3 victories.
• 1978 - Ben won Lyme Park novice.
• 1978-79 - Nursery - Nil
• 1979 - Ben won Nelson, Rydal, Trawden, Hayfield. Spot won Marple Bridge, Oldham, Heighington.
• 1979-80 - Nursery - Roy won 9 awards with 4 victories inc. Holme Champ. Cap won 9 awards with 4 victories inc. Trawden Champ.

qualifying - 4th in Supreme, Cardiff. Vic won Royal Lancs, Oldham, Abbeystead. Fleet and Clyde won Burnley and Royal Lancs brace.
• 1971-2 Nursery - Sweep (son of Fleet) won 16 awards with 6 victories inc. Inter-Club championship.
• 1972 - Fleet won Burnley, Winton - 5th in National - 2nd in International qualifying (reserve International Farmer's champion) - 4th Supreme. Clyde won Nelson, Quernmore, Leek - 10th in National - 10th in International qualifying - 9th supreme. Vic won Royal Lancs. Fleet and Clyde 2nd National brace - 5th International.
• 1972-73 Nursery - Sally won 2 awards with 1 victory.
• 1973 - Fleet won Macclesfield Forest. Clyde won Wexford in Ireland. Clyde 4th in National at Rydal - 9th in International qualifying - 2nd in Supreme. Fleet and Clyde won International Brace Championship. 2nd in National.
• 1973-74 Nursery - Fly 3 awards - Jock 2 awards

• 1980 - Roy won Dent.
• 1980-81 - Nursery - Nil.
• 1981 - Cap I 11th at National - 25th International qualifying. No other victories that year.
• 1981-82 - Nursery - Cap 1 award.
• 1982 - Cap I won Caton. 5th in National - 15 in International. Qualifying - 9th Supreme.
• 1982-83 - Nursery - Rock 1 award.
• 1983 - Lad won Yorkshire open championship.
• 1983-84 - Nursery - Nil
• 1984 - Lad won Littleborough.
• 1984-85 - Nursery - Nil
• 1985 - Cap II won Hayfield, Royal Lancs, opens and Yorkshire novice.
• 1985-86 Nursery - Scott won 23 awards, incl. 11 victories and the champs. of Trawden, Meltham, Holme, Rossendale. Moss won 1 award.
• 1986 - Cap I won Harden Moss, Lyme, 6th in National - 23rd Int. qualifying. Cap II won Rossendale, Royal Lancs championship - English National Champion - 32nd in Int. Qual. Cap I

Early days at Holme in Cliviger Open. Left to right: Unknown, J Wilkinson (Whistler), Eric Halsall, P Connern, B Moore, Jim with Fleet, J Reed, D Hutchinson and nephew, H Todd.

Another picture from the Holme in Cliviger Open. Left to right: Front: Alf Kyme with Gary, Jim with Cap I, Danny Wild, J Gumbley; Back: J Heap, R Wild, Eric Halsall.

and Cap II won Royal Lancs, Lyme, brace - 2nd in National - 5th in International.

• 1986-87 Nursery - Ben won 14 awards inc. 4 victories and Northern Society Champ.

• 1987 - Ben won Garstang, Dent, Hope. 10th in National. Cap II won Holme.

• 1987-88 Nursery - Bill 4 awards - Tex 1 award.

• 1987 (shown in 1988) - Cap I and Cap II won One Man and His Dog brace.

• 1988 - Cap II won Bodfari, Rossendale, Lunesdale, Hayfield champ. 6th in National. Ben won Lyme, Hornby, National Ploughing trials.

• 1988-89 Nursery - Bracken 1 award - Shep 8 awards inc. 2 victories and Inter-Club champ.

• 1989 - Cap II won Derwent Hill, Holme, Trawden, Meltham. Ben won Lowgill.

• 1989-90 Nursery - Roy 12 awards inc. 8 victories. Jac 11 awards inc. 4 victories.

• 1990 - Cap II won Ketton, Douglas (Isle of Man), Lowgill, Thirsk, Cowpe. Ben won Bodfari, Lymm, Hambleton. Shep won Garstang, Littleborough School, Scar Sykes Hill, Deerplay Hill, Royal Lancs champ. Rossendale Lions.

• 1990 - 91 Nursery - to date (12.1.91) - Mirk 9 awards inc. 1 victory.

# Useful Contacts

Dick Roper, Jim and Toddy Lambe talking in Ireland in 2004, where Jim won the European Championship title.

Although you can own a Border Collie without being a member of the International Sheep Dog Society, you cannot register any pups, or enter National Trials, without joining. To join, simply contact ISDS at Clifton House, 4a Goldington Road, Bedford, UK. MK40 3NF.

The next question is to decide on Annual or Life Membership. For many, the latter is the better alternative, and those who became 'Lifers' years ago are now pleased with their bargain. Membership fees tend to edge upwards, so Life Membership could be a sound investment.

Either way, there is a good return on your money. You will be sent lists of entries into the National Trials, and gain entrance tickets and car stickers at preferential rates.

Through 'International Sheepdog News' you will be able to keep up to date with happenings in the sheep dog world, trial dates, and lists of dogs for sale and wanted through its bi-monthly colourful pages. If you want to buy a bitch or select a stud dog, there will be ample choice advertised. You will have the right to attend the Annual General Meeting, staged during each National. ISDS also produces an annual Stud Book and, though

expensive, these become indispensable to the serious breeder and are an appreciating asset.

Choosing a dog is dealt with in an earlier chapter. You don't have to follow fashions, and the top handlers are not necessarily the best models for the novice. They may well choose a dog with a bit of 'tiger' in it, to mould to their own ways. The beginner needs something a bit easier and softer. Lady handlers usually want something a bit kinder. Female triallists were once the exception, but today they are getting far too good!

If you know no one in the sheep dog world, ISDS will be more than ready to help, sending a list of breeders in your particular area. If you want a registered pup, its breeder must be an ISDS member, and he should register the animal for you. You should select a name, so that it can be added to the registration form.

Some breeders have a prefix. This has to be approved by ISDS, as it must not clash with prefixes already registered. Shirley and I use Irwell, because a spring in the back field here is the source of the River Irwell, which becomes a substantial feature further down country. Many famous prefixes spring to mind; Wiston, for ever to be associated with Wiston Cap; Mindrum, used by that great shepherd, Bob Fraser, and Bosworth, for Bosworth Coon.

The breeder pays the registration fee, and usually includes it in his price! He has to complete a book with spaces for ten puppies, and it must be done within the stated number of weeks after birth, or fines are payable. The breeder sends the whole book, so may wait till all names are obtained. You will be sent details of the dog's parentage, and now is the time to obtain its five-generation pedigree. That is something you can work out for yourself, if you have sufficient stud books. There is no more pleasurable occupation on a winter's evening, as you may well come across unexpected famous names, winners of trials long ago. A number of enterprising people now advertise five generation pedigrees, which undoubtedly save a lot of time.

BREEDING

The time may come when you wish to breed a litter. According to ISDS rules the owner of the dog has to send in a Mating Card to the Society.

When the litter is born, the puppies must be registered if you wish to continue with the pedigree. On receipt of the mating card, the Society will send a Puppy Registration Book with pages for ten pups. Each page has the outline of a puppy, which you must fill in as accurately as possible. Draw in the markings on both sides, and indicate the colour; black, red, merle or tan.

Up to six months from the birth date of the litter is allowed for this, but don't leave it to the last moment. It is all too easy to defer, and then you suddenly come up against the deadline and a hefty fine. Do all the drawings at the same time, covering the whole litter, and post it off with the appropriate fee.

The registration forms then come back to the breeder, who distributes each to the puppy's new owners.

SALES

When buying or selling a dog, a Transfer of Ownership form must be filled in, and signed by the vendor. A fee is payable, and vendor and buyer must be clear about who is paying. After the transfer, ISDS will send a Registration Certificate to the new owner, with their name on it.

If a dog dies, the Registration Certificate should be returned to the Society. However, not many do.

Another piece of clerical work is to enter the trial of your choice. You will see the trial advertised, certainly in 'International Sheepdog News', and you contact the secretary by post, phone or email. After two years' entries, most secretaries will remind you automatically.

# Pedigrees

A selection of pedigrees of some of Jim's and Shirley's most notable dogs, compiled by Teun van den Dool.

Bonnie, Clyde and Fleet share the same breeding. This is Fleet's pedigree:

**Fleet  38813**, dog, smooth, B&W, born 27-04-1965, CI6 = 6.1% (high, line-bred), 229 registered children from 58 litters.
owner: J.Cropper,  1972 IntSu 4th, 1972 IntQ 2nd

| Parents | Grand-Parents | G.G.-Parents | G.G.G.-Parents | G.G.G.G.-Parents |
|---|---|---|---|---|
| Rock 27425 J.H.T.Bathgate | Hope 13418 R.L.Hardie | Hope 7029 J.Anderson 1953 IntSu 5th | Garry 4915 J.Anderson | Glen 3957, S.Banks |
| | | | | Tib 4458, S.Banks |
| | | | Biddy 5492 J.Anderson | Cap 3036, J.M.Wilson |
| | | | | Meg 2787, J.R.Hislop |
| | | Tib 8658 W.Falconer | Spot 7320 J.H.T.Gilchrist 1956 IntSu 5th | Roy 5323, W.D.Renwick |
| | | | | Jed 4941, J.A.S.Gilchrist |
| | | | Meg 6915 P.Brotherstone | Glen 3868, J.Hogarth |
| | | | | Floss 5636, G.Brotherston |
| | Mist 14246 A.D.R.Cockburn | Tweed 9601 J.M.Wilson 1958 IntSu 1st | Moss 5176 J.M.Wilson 1949 IntSu 2nd | Mirk 4438, J.M.Wilson, 1950 IntSu 1st |
| | | | | Nell 3514, J.Kirk |
| | | | Trim 8859 R.Anderson | Spot II 6775, W.R.Little, 1954 S.Nat 1st |
| | | | | Phil 6132, W.R.Little |
| | | Trim 7552 A.D.R.Cockburn | Nap 3732 T.Lothian | Cap 3036, J.M.Wilson |
| | | | | Meg 3640, D.F.Lothian |
| | | | Nell 6879 (ROM) Wm.J.Evans 1951 IntSu 2nd | Moss 6811, A.Jones, 1952 IntSu 2nd |
| | | | | Ffy (NR), R.Wood |
| Trim 26864 J.Bonella | Bill II 17937 J.M.Wilson MBE | Whitehope Nap 8685 J.M.Wilson 1955 IntSu 2nd | Glen 6123 W.McClure | Mark 4991, J.T.Jones |
| | | | | Floss 5058, J.T.Jones |
| | | | Meg 5141 W.E.McClure 1953 IntSu 12th | Jim (NR), Mr.Scott |
| | | | | Nell 3514, J.Kirk |
| | | Meg 12223 J.C.Howie | Moss 5176 J.M.Wilson 1949 IntSu 2nd | Mirk 4438, J.M.Wilson, 1950 IntSu 1st |
| | | | | Nell 3514, J.Kirk |
| | | | Trim 8859 R.Anderson | Spot II 6775, W.R.Little, 1954 S.Nat 1st |
| | | | | Phil 6132, W.R.Little |
| | Tib 21675 J.Bonella | Dan 12730 W.Bell | Speed 4382 J.R.Millar 1952 IntSu 4th | Roy (NR), J.Paton |
| | | | | Emma (NR), D.McCutcheon |
| | | | Nell 7512 Mrs.A.L.McCormack | Moss 5176, J.M.Wilson, 1949 IntSu 2nd |
| | | | | Nan 7501, J.R.Hislop |
| | | Trim 13771 J.M.Wilson | Tweed 9601 J.M.Wilson 1958 IntSu 1st | Moss 5176, J.M.Wilson, 1949 IntSu 2nd |
| | | | | Trim 8859, R.Anderson |
| | | | Phill II 6631 J.M.Wilson | Speed 4382, J.R.Millar, 1952 IntSu 4th |
| | | | | Phil 5980, J.B.Simpson |

Cap I (aka Fonzi) was one of the famous pair which won the One Man and His Dog Brace competition in 1987:

**Cap  108026**, dog, rough, B,W&T, born 09-03-1978, CI6 = 0.7% (low, out-cross), 15 registered children from 3 litters.
owner: J.Cropper,  1982 IntSu 9th, 1982 E.Nat 5th

| Parents | Grand-Parents | G.G.-Parents | G.G.G.-Parents | G.G.G.G.-Parents |
|---|---|---|---|---|
| Moss 59810 A.Redfearn | Craig 47703 T.Watson 1970 IntQ 2nd | Mirk 35066 T.Watson | Jim 26534 T.Watson | Craig 21227, D.McTeir |
| | | | | Nell II 18491, J.G.Brownlie |
| | | | Nell 29636 J.F.Bradbury | Shep 18504, T.Watson |
| | | | | Mindrum Jill 18496, R.S.Fraser |
| | | June 30402 A.Livingstone | Garry 19382 A.Chapman 1966 S.Nat 3rd | Cap 7594, J.Walker |
| | | | | Nell 15388, J.Kirk |
| | | | Tip 13416 A.Chapman | Cap 10910, M.Jones |
| | | | | Sue 12082, S.Howarth |
| | Maid 46597 A.Noble | Spot 24981 J.Gilchrist 1966 IntSu 2nd | Bob 12684 J.A.S.Gilchrist 1963 S.Br 2nd | Spot 7320, J.A.S.Gilchrist, 1956 IntSu 5th |
| | | | | Nell 10141, G.Hunter |
| | | | Wiston Nan III 9896 P.M.Hepburn | Moss 5176, J.M.Wilson, 1949 IntSu 2nd |
| | | | | Ann 4545, W.S.Hetherington |
| | | Queen 16968 A.Noble | Mindrum Jeff 14422 T.Watson | Tam 8279, T.Watson |
| | | | | Mindrum Nell 11106, R.S.Fraser, 1955 E.Sh 1st |
| | | | Queen 12652 P.H.Jaffray | Dave 7900, T.Wilson, 1953 IntSu 2nd |
| | | | | Nell 10867, T.F.Courtney |
| Fly 53163 J.C.Clarke | Vic II 17569 E.Humphreys | Vic 10928 Wm.Sanderson | Patch 6531 T.S.Roberts | Sweep 4702, G.Pugh |
| | | | | Jess 5177, T.S.Roberts |
| | | | Moni 8788 E.P.Evans | Vic 4368, D.H.Murray, 1952 IntSu 3rd |
| | | | | Mona 6091, A.McPhee |
| | | Queen II 11541 B.Holmes | Hope 7029 J.Anderson 1953 IntSu 5th | Garry 4915, J.Anderson |
| | | | | Biddy 5492, J.Anderson |
| | | | Maid 10892 D.T.Brotherstone | Hemp 8822, T.H.Johnston |
| | | | | Jed 9183, D.T.Brotherstone |
| | Fan 37233 E.Humphreys | Spot 23845 L.Roberts | Moss 18885 H.G.Jones | Spot 5530, R.H.Williams |
| | | | | Moni 8788, R.E.Roberts |
| | | | Wendy II 13195 H.G.Jones | Ben 11401 (ROM), Wm.Jones, 1959 IntSu 3rd |
| | | | | Wendy 11972, C.Holmes |
| | | Fly 17341 E.Humphreys | Roy 14989 A.Owen | Jeff 13348, L.Greenwood |
| | | | | Juno II 11270, L.Greenwood |
| | | | Fly 15862 E.Humphreys | Ben 6339, J.Holmes |
| | | | | Wendy 11972, C.Holmes |

Deerplay on a windy day.

Cap II was the other member of that Brace team:

**Cap 142018**, dog, rough,B&W, born 04-09-1983, CI6 = 3.3% (average, normal), 255 registered children from 52 litters.
owner: J.Cropper, 1986 E.Nat 1st, 1986 E.Br 2nd

| Parents | Grand-Parents | G.G.-Parents | G.G.G.-Parents | G.G.G.G.-Parents |
|---|---|---|---|---|
| **Dryden Joe 104626**<br>R.Dalziel<br>1986 S.Nat 1st | **Glen 75630**<br>R.Fortune<br>1977 S.Nat 11th | **Cap 67230**<br>T.T.McKnight | **Cap 52841**<br>A.M.C.Rogerson | Mindrum Corrie 31439, R.S.Fraser, 1968 IntSh 1st |
| | | | | Midge 33950, A.M.C.Rogerson |
| | | | **Lassie 60521**<br>T.T.McKnight | Jaff 38313, T.T.McKnight, 1969 S.Br 1st |
| | | | | Jill 41933, J.C.Hetterick |
| | | **Shell 68768**<br>T.T.McKnight | **Drift 51202** T.T.McKnight<br>1970 IntDr 1st | Jaff 38313, T.T.McKnight, 1969 S.Br 1st |
| | | | | Dot III 18925, T.T.McKnight, 1967 IntSu 2nd |
| | | | **Shell 56986** J.D.Robinson<br>1973 S.Nat 7th | Ben 47543 (ROM), R.Bailey |
| | | | | Nell 46736, A.H.Tait |
| | **Dryden Queen 70345**<br>A.D.MacGregor | **Spot 24981**<br>J.Gilchrist<br>1966 IntSu 2nd | **Bob 12684** J.A.S.Gilchrist<br>1963 S.Br 2nd | Spot 7320, J.A.S.Gilchrist, 1956 IntSu 5th |
| | | | | Nell 10141, G.Hunter |
| | | | **Wiston Nan III 9896**<br>P.M.Hepburn | Moss 5176, J.M.Wilson, 1949 IntSu 2nd |
| | | | | Ann 4545, W.S.Hetherington |
| | | **Chris 60920**<br>A.D.MacGregor | **Scot 28069** G.Wm.Young<br>1969 IntSh 1st | Hemp 21291, Mrs.G.Wood |
| | | | | Midge 17786, G.Wm.Young |
| | | | **Phil 24983**<br>P.M.G.Hepburn | Bob 12684, J.A.S.Gilchrist |
| | | | | Wiston Nan III 9896, P.M.Hepburn |
| **Floss 88122**<br>J.Hawkins | **Fleet 38813**<br>J.Cropper<br>1972 IntSu 4th | **Rock 27425**<br>J.H.T.Bathgate | **Hope 13418**<br>R.L.Hardie | Hope 7029, J.Anderson, 1953 IntSu 5th |
| | | | | Tib 8658, W.Falconer |
| | | | **Mist 14246**<br>A.D.R.Cockburn | Tweed 9601, J.M.Wilson, 1958 IntSu 1st |
| | | | | Trim 7552, A.D.R.Cockburn |
| | | **Trim 26864**<br>J.Bonella | **Bill II 17937**<br>J.M.Wilson MBE | Whitehope Nap 8685, J.M.Wilson, 1955 IntSu 2nd |
| | | | | Meg 12223, J.C.Howie |
| | | | **Tib 21675**<br>J.Bonella | Dan 12730, W.Bell |
| | | | | Trim 13771, J.M.Wilson |
| | **Wychnor-Hope 73538**<br>J.Hawkins | **Mirk 28776**<br>J.C.Hettrick<br>1971 S.Nat 1st | **Cap 13274**<br>M.Wm.Cook | Cap 4295, M.Collin, 1951 IntBr 1st |
| | | | | Lassie 10680, M.Wm.Cook |
| | | | **Gael 14463** T.T.McKnight<br>1967 IntSu 1st | Whitehope Nap 8685, J.M.Wilson, 1955 IntSu 2nd |
| | | | | Dot 11228, T.T.McKnight |
| | | **Gael 57306**<br>E.Kelly | **Spot 24981** J.Gilchrist<br>1966 IntSu 2nd | Bob 12684, J.A.S.Gilchrist |
| | | | | Wiston Nan III 9896, P.M.Hepburn |
| | | | **Dot 51922**<br>J.Hawkins | Glen 16214, W.D.Ewin |
| | | | | Dot 25580, G.L.Hutton |

Now for three of Jim's more recent dogs:

**Alf 256928**, dog, medium,B,W&T, born 26-08-2001, CI6 = 1.0% (low, out-cross)
owner: J.Cropper, 2003 E.Br 3th

| Parents | Grand-Parents | G.G.-Parents | G.G.G.-Parents | G.G.G.G.-Parents |
|---|---|---|---|---|
| **Moss 173999**<br>A.Kyme<br>1994 E.Nat 13th | **Moel Craig 150776**<br>Wm.R.Roberts<br>1988 W.Nat 5th | **Carl 107085**<br>R.B.Scrivener | **Mirk 78560**<br>T.A.Quayle | Tos 61152, Capt.A.G.Jones, 1974 W.Nat 1st |
| | | | | Bet 52164, J.A.Jones |
| | | | **Gwen 94671**<br>T.A.Quayle | Mindrum-Cap II 73216, R.D.Kinrade, 1975 I.Nat 2nd |
| | | | | Meg 66811, R.W.Kinvig |
| | | **Lyn 125926**<br>Miss C.S.Jones | **Bwlch Taff 113243** H.G.Jones<br>1982 IntSu 2nd | Glen 92091, H.G.Jones, 1977 IntQ 4th |
| | | | | Bwlch Bracken 74660, Mrs.B.M.Jones, 1977 W.Br 1st |
| | | | **Tess 94003**<br>J.E.Hughes | Nap 69487, I.S.Stirling |
| | | | | Gale 72143, J.Gray |
| | **Meg 152389**<br>R.G.Davies | **Elian Jaff 125519**<br>R.Davies | **Risp 117139**<br>E.N.Davies | Moss 91079, T.J.Bowey |
| | | | | Spey 99226, Wm.Ellwood |
| | | | **Nel 98448**<br>M.Ll.Hughes | Sweep 84612, D.Owen |
| | | | | Meg II 73654, J.E.Ritchie |
| | | **Jill 136584**<br>R.G.Jones | **Rhaiadr Zac 94341**<br>Miss A.Edwards | Rex 78894, A.Jones |
| | | | | Rhaiadr Fly 81521, E.Humphreys |
| | | | **Jill 118825**<br>R.Davies | Mirk 52844, G.Lloyd, 1970 IntQ 1st |
| | | | | Tess 92026, R.Davies |
| **Molly 251622**<br>A.Kyme | **Davey 235474**<br>Miss M.Ingham | **Clifton Bill 201460**<br>J.P.Mason | **Don 141536** E.W.Edwards<br>1992 IntSu 4th | Bill 78263, E.W.Edwards, 1982 IntSu 1st |
| | | | | Fly 125053, A.Owen |
| | | | **Sally 177236**<br>Mrs.N.A.Harrison | Dryden Spam 112653, J.M.Perrings, 1985 E.Nat 2nd |
| | | | | Tess 155989, L.N.Harrison |
| | | **Midge 173081**<br>D.Wood | **Sweep 140188**<br>A.J.Bland | Clint 130309 (ROM), R.Fielden |
| | | | | Mist 117023, R.Fielden |
| | | | **Lassie 157892**<br>A.J.Bland | Sam 143963, R.Bradley |
| | | | | Nan 120963, C.T.Ennion |
| | **Jess 238557**<br>A.Kyme | **Spot 214428**<br>H.Mee | **Roy 186355**<br>Wm.Miller | Spot 127763, Wm.Miller |
| | | | | Bess 148173, A.R.Hunter |
| | | | **Jan 198855**<br>Wm.Miller | Black 144068, J.E.Lightfoot, 1991 W.Nat 1st |
| | | | | Nip 173146, R.P.Dean, 1995 E.Br 1st |
| | | **Meg 199091**<br>H.Mee | **Tan 178000**<br>R.H.Hunter | Black 144068, J.E.Lightfoot, 1991 W.Nat 1st |
| | | | | Queen 128899, J.Hawkins |
| | | | **Nell 183098**<br>Wm.Miller | Rhys 155535, Mrs.S.Walker |
| | | | | Meg 170453, Wm.Miller |

**Dan  258392**, dog, smooth,B&W, born 30-11-2001, CI6 = 0.8% (low, out-cross)
owner: J.Cropper,  2003 E.Br 3th

| Parents | Grand-Parents | G.G.-Parents | G.G.G.-Parents | G.G.G.G.-Parents |
|---|---|---|---|---|
| **Sid 244412** J.Cropper 2002 WorldCh 2nd | **Bwlch Hemp 201604** Mrs.C.S.Rundle 1996 W.Nat 13th | **Ben 129820** A.Owen 1985 IntSu 3th | **Rhaiadr Zac 94341** Miss A.Edwards | **Rex 78894**, A.Jones |
| | | | | **Rhaiadr Fly 81521**, E.Humphreys |
| | | | **Fan 102412** R.Williams | **Moss 84044**, S.Jones |
| | | | | **Meg 71772**, W.T.Williams |
| | | **Dell 172782** Mrs.B.M.Jones | **Bwlch Taff 113243** Miss C.S.Jones, 1982 IntSu 2nd | **Glen 92091**, H.G.Jones, 1977 IntQ 4th |
| | | | | **Bwlch Bracken 74660**, Mrs.B.M.Jones, 1977 W.Br 1st |
| | | | **Bonny 136053** W.A.L.Prothero | **Ben 73508**, R.Wood |
| | | | | **Jen 124917**, D.J.Rees |
| | **Jet 226549** L.N.Watkins | **Craig 212955** J.G.Grant | **Jos 152124** J.R.Thomas 1988 E.Nat 4th | **Dilwyn Lad II 100895**, J.R.Thomas |
| | | | | **Dell 136052**, R.C.Barwell |
| | | | **Rhosfa Jill 183614** J.G.Grant | **Bwlch Taff 113243**, Miss C.S.Jones, 1982 IntSu 2nd |
| | | | | **Gypsy 130307**, D.J.Rees |
| | | **Joy 185629** J.G.Grant | **Laddie 160443** J.Dixon | **Dryden Joe 104626**, R.Dalziel, 1986 S.Nat 1st |
| | | | | **Chriss 101746**, R.Neill |
| | | | **Mey 167928** J.G.Grant | **Glen 143941**, J.F.McRobert, 1990 IntSu 3th |
| | | | | **Nell 157613**, J.F.McRobert |
| **Gail 251180** S.Richards | **Joe 205312** Miss K.Gibson | **Glen 168524** W.T.A.Goligher 1997 W.Nat 2nd | **York 127630**  J.Paterson 1983 S.Nat 3th | **Glen 75630**, R.Fortune |
| | | | | **Dot 99192**, T.M.Hutchinson |
| | | | **Di 137205** J.H.Porteous | **Moss 103923**, J.J.Templeton MBE, 1979 IntSu 2nd |
| | | | | **Lassie 80703**, D.L.Porteous Jnr. |
| | | **Jet 178683** Mrs.S.Gibson | **Kelly 159648** W.T.A.Goligher | **Jim 125956**, D.J.Brady |
| | | | | **Judy 128986**, L.Kelly |
| | | | **Nan 170569** W.T.A.Goligher | **Sweep 127047**, W.J.M.McGoldrick, 1984 I.Nat 4th |
| | | | | **Bute 153154**, W.C.Hemphill |
| | **Joy 231169** A.J.Palmer | **Cap 185676** A.J.Palmer 1995 IntSu 7th | **Fleet II 135475** A.J.Palmer | **Jim 125233**, A.Bradley |
| | | | | **Gael 96527**, D.France |
| | | | **Tess 161020** R.A.Shepherd | **Don 108889**, J.R.Thomas, 1982 IntSu 5th |
| | | | | **Meg 130497**, J.N.Wheaton |
| | | **Tib 210707** W.M.Buchanan | **Craig 191917** G.Pringle | **Nap 175718**, C.A.Smart |
| | | | | **Dot 162411**, C.A.Smart |
| | | | **Meg 190395** J.W.Nesbit | **Taff 140712**, C.Scott |
| | | | | **Shell 174677**, J.Dickinson |

**Sid  244412**, dog, smooth,B&W, born 15-04-1999, CI6 = 3.7% (average, normal), 138 registered children from 21 litters.
owner: J.Cropper,  2002 WorldCh 2nd, 2002 E.Nat 7th

| Parents | Grand-Parents | G.G.-Parents | G.G.G.-Parents | G.G.G.G.-Parents |
|---|---|---|---|---|
| **Bwlch Hemp 201604** Mrs.C.S.Rundle 1996 W.Nat 13th | **Ben 129820** A.Owen 1985 IntSu 3th | **Rhaiadr Zac 94341** Miss A.Edwards | **Rex 78894**  A.Jones 1974 W.Nat 5th | **Roy 44716**, J.G.Jones |
| | | | | **Meed 72955**, J.G.Jones |
| | | | **Rhaiadr Fly 81521** E.Humphreys | **Wiston Cap 31154**, R.J.Richardson, 1965 IntSu 1st |
| | | | | **Gael 63451**, E.Humphreys |
| | | **Fan 102412** R.Williams | **Moss 84044**  S.Jones 1978 W.Nat 5th | **Wiston Cap 31154**, R.J.Richardson, 1965 IntSu 1st |
| | | | | **Gyp 56601**, T.W.Longton, 1977 E.Nat 2nd |
| | | | **Meg 71772** W.T.Williams | **Craig 47577**, E.A.Griffith |
| | | | | **Nell 43755**, W.T.Williams |
| | **Dell 172782** Mrs.B.M.Jones | **Bwlch Taff 113243** Miss C.S.Jones 1982 IntSu 2nd | **Glen 92091**  H.G.Jones 1977 IntQ 4th | **Glen 62253 (ROM)**, D.MacDonald, 1974 S.Nat 1st |
| | | | | **Lass 62964**, D.MacDonald |
| | | | **Bwlch Bracken 74660** Mrs.B.M.Jones, 1977 W.Br 1st | **Wiston Cap 31154**, R.J.Richardson, 1965 IntSu 1st |
| | | | | **Sheba 33229**, Mrs.B.M.Jones |
| | | **Bonny 136053** W.A.L.Prothero | **Ben 73508** R.Wood | **Wiston Cap 31154**, R.J.Richardson, 1965 IntSu 1st |
| | | | | **Liz 37009**, R.Wood, 1974 IntSu 3th |
| | | | **Jen 124917** D.J.Rees | **Don 108889**, J.R.Thomas, 1982 IntSu 5th |
| | | | | **Dell 70443**, W.R.Hughes |
| **Jet 226549** L.N.Watkins | **Craig 212955** J.G.Grant | **Jos 152124** J.R.Thomas 1988 E.Nat 4th | **Dilwyn Lad II 100895** J.R.Thomas | **Craig 59425**, J.R.Thomas, 1977 IntSu 1st |
| | | | | **Bet 66184**, H.G.J.Havard |
| | | | **Dell 136052** R.C.Barwell | **Ben 73508**, R.Wood |
| | | | | **Jen 124917**, D.J.Rees |
| | | **Rhosfa Jill 183614** J.G.Grant | **Bwlch Taff 113243** Miss C.S.Jones, 1982 IntSu 2nd | **Glen 92091**, H.G.Jones, 1977 IntQ 4th |
| | | | | **Bwlch Bracken 74660**, Mrs.B.M.Jones, 1977 W.Br 1st |
| | | | **Gypsy 130307** D.J.Rees | **Rob 87667**, C.Cook |
| | | | | **Nell 100677**, C.Cook |
| | **Joy 185629** J.G.Grant | **Laddie 160443** J.Dixon | **Dryden Joe 104626**  R.Dalziel 1986 S.Nat 1st | **Glen 75630**, R.Fortune |
| | | | | **Dryden Queen 70345**, A.D.MacGregor |
| | | | **Chriss 101746** R.Neill | **Tam 83093**, R.S.Short |
| | | | | **Nell 93150**, R.S.Short |
| | | **Mey 167928** J.G.Grant | **Glen 143941**  J.F.McRobert 1990 IntSu 3th | **Mirk III 120673**, A.S.MacRae, 1985 S.Nat 4th |
| | | | | **Nell 131110**, Wm.Wilson |
| | | | **Nell 157613** J.F.McRobert | **Dryden Joe 104626**, R.Dalziel, 1986 S.Nat 1st |
| | | | | **Fly 140899**, S.Anderson |

And, finally, three of Shirley's dogs:

**Beechwood Bob 230975**, dog, rough,B,W&T, born 01-04-1997, CI6 = 2.6% (average, normal), 41 children from 8 litters.
owner: Mrs.S.Cropper, 2003 E.Nat 3th

| Parents | Grand-Parents | G.G.-Parents | G.G.G.-Parents | G.G.G.G.-Parents |
|---|---|---|---|---|
| **Clifton Rob 201456**<br><br>T.Longton<br><br>1997 E.Nat 5th | **Don 141536**<br>E.W.Edwards<br>1992 IntSu 4th | **Bill 78263**<br>E.W.Edwards<br>1982 IntSu 1st | **Bill 51654** Sir E.G.Jones<br>1974 IntSu 1st | **Wiston Cap 31154**, J.R.Richardson, 1965 IntSu 1st |
| | | | | **Nan 21068**, W.Kinstrey |
| | | | **R. Fly 59282**<br>Mrs.M.K.Jones | **Fleet 38813**, J.Cropper, 1972 IntSu 4th |
| | | | | **Gail 42493**, Wm.Robinson |
| | | **Fly 125053**<br>A.Owen | **Craig 72737** A.Jones<br>1977 IntSu 2nd | **Moss 57707**, A.Jones |
| | | | | **Nell 61154**, D.Owen |
| | | | **Jess 96742**<br>A.Owen | **Cap 80822**, R.E.Nicholls, 1977 W.Nat 4th |
| | | | | **Jill 66841**, R.E.Nicholls |
| | **Sally 177236**<br>Mrs.N.A.Harrison | **Dryden Spam 112653**<br>J.M.Perrings<br>1985 E.Nat 2nd | **Glen 75630**<br>R.Fortune | **Cap 67230**, T.T.McKnight |
| | | | | **Shell 68768**, T.T.McKnight |
| | | | **Dryden Queen 70345**<br>A.D.MacGregor | **Spot 24981**, J.Gilchrist, 1966 IntSu 2nd |
| | | | | **Chris 60920**, A.D.MacGregor |
| | | **Tess 155989**<br>L.N.Harrison | **Nap 107731**<br>S.Hodgkinson | **Jim 96950**, J.M.E.Jack |
| | | | | **Nell 60038**, A.M.McMillan |
| | | | **Fan 135124**<br>W.R.Ormiston | **Rodney 122905**, R.E.Nicholls |
| | | | | **Queen 82050**, J.J.Nicholls |
| **Meg 188856**<br><br>N.A.Bennett | **Cap 142018**<br>J.Cropper<br>1986 E.Nat 1st | **Dryden Joe 104626**<br>R.Dalziel<br>1986 S.Nat 1st | **Glen 75630**<br>R.Fortune | **Cap 67230**, T.T.McKnight |
| | | | | **Shell 68768**, T.T.McKnight |
| | | | **Dryden Queen 70345**<br>A.D.MacGregor | **Spot 24981**, J.Gilchrist, 1966 IntSu 2nd |
| | | | | **Chris 60920**, A.D.MacGregor |
| | | **Floss 88122**<br>J.Hawkins | **Fleet 38813** J.Cropper<br>1972 IntSu 4th | **Rock 27425**, J.H.T.Bathgate |
| | | | | **Trim 26864**, J.Bonella |
| | | | **Wychnor-Hope 73538**<br>J.Hawkins | **Mirk 28776**, J.C.Hettrick, 1971 S.Nat 1st |
| | | | | **Gael 57306**, E.Kelly |
| | **Lassie 163542**<br>J.G.Barnes | **Glen 137733**<br>E.A.Griffith | **Bwlch Taff 113243** H.G.Jones<br>1982 IntSu 2nd | **Glen 92091**, H.G.Jones, 1977 IntQ 4th |
| | | | | **Bwlch Bracken 74660**, Mrs.B.M.Jones, 1977 W.Br 1st |
| | | | **Jess 120408**<br>C.Williams | **Gel 104284**, H.G.Jones |
| | | | | **Nell 106926**, I.Jones |
| | | **Jess 146763**<br>G.Owen | **Linton Scott 93681**<br>J.D.Williams | **Garry II 72575**, D.McTeir |
| | | | | **Lassie 80954**, R.T.D.Gibson |
| | | | **Meg 103354**<br>G.Owen | **Craig 47577**, E.A.Griffith |
| | | | | **Bet 52164**, J.A.Jones |

**Lilly 264162**, bitch, rough,B&W, born 18-04-2003, CI6 = 0.1% (low, out-cross)
owner: Mrs.S.Cropper

| Parents | Grand-Parents | G.G.-Parents | G.G.G.-Parents | G.G.G.G.-Parents |
|---|---|---|---|---|
| **Cap**<br>**250756**<br><br>E.Baxter<br><br>2004 IntQ 4th | **Rob**<br>**200948**<br>T.H.Longton<br>1997 E.Nat 2nd | **Cap 161769**<br>T.Longton Jnr.<br>1990 E.Br 1st | **Dryden Spam 112653**<br>J.M.Perrings, 1985 E.Nat 2nd | **Glen 75630**, R.Fortune |
| | | | | **Dryden Queen 70345**, A.D.MacGregor |
| | | | **Gel 124181** T.Longton Jnr.<br>1990 E.Br 1st | **Blade 78505**, C.W.Storey |
| | | | | **Tib 78130**, E.Wass |
| | | **Becca 170072**<br>T.Longton<br>1993 IntBr 2nd | **Chip 151557**<br>W.G.Beddows | **Davy 131049**, S.B.Price, 1987 IntSu 1st |
| | | | | **Jen 137392**, S.B.Price |
| | | | **Becca 145672**<br>J.Beaman | **Ben 123761**, J.E.James, 1986 E.Nat 2nd |
| | | | | **Biddy 138136 (ROM)**, R.W.F.Renshaw |
| | **Meg**<br>**242074**<br>N.Brown | **Roy 215260**<br>D.M.A.Lee | **Hilston Snap 174335**<br>W.R.Ormiston | **Flash 137604**, A.G.Heaton |
| | | | | **Whitethorne Snip 118855**, G.P.Blyth |
| | | | **Trim 173393**<br>W.R.Ormiston | **Cap 136263**, G.W.Billingham |
| | | | | **Meg 139973**, T.J.Davidson |
| | | **Bess 232515**<br>D.T.Evans | **Lad 214439** M.Ll.Evans<br>1998 W.Nat 1st | **Mirk 167213**, R.E.Jones |
| | | | | **Fan 194518**, H.G.Williams |
| | | | **Bet 189759**<br>E.B.Roberts | **Mac 116944**, Wm.D.Jones |
| | | | | **Jill 157699**, R.E.Roberts |
| **Udale Rosebud**<br>**226403**<br><br>E.Baxter | **Andy**<br>**166124**<br>J.M.Hutchinson | **Moss 131207**<br>R.A.Elliot<br>1984 E.Nat 1st | **Cap 97169**<br>S.P.Walton | **Shep 67185**, K.W.Shield, 1974 E.Nat 4th |
| | | | | **Jed 79816**, K.W.Shield |
| | | | **Langloch Nell 84216**<br>A.Elliott | **Jim 64812**, J.Davidson |
| | | | | **Nell 64328**, J.Davidson |
| | | **Meg 135478**<br>D.France | **Jim 125233**<br>A.Bradley | **Bob 70372**, H.Mee |
| | | | | **Gwen 100714**, A.Bradley |
| | | | **Gael 96527**<br>D.France | **Cap 67230**, C.W.Relph |
| | | | | **Spy 63616**, D.France |
| | **Udale Lassie**<br>**174673**<br>H.Huddleston | **Bill 134009**<br>J.F.Marston | **Craig 120426**<br>H.Rowlands | **Craig 59425**, J.R.Thomas, 1977 IntSu 1st |
| | | | | **Jill 102583**, H.Rowlands |
| | | | **Meg 118615**<br>Mrs.D.Roberts | **Roy 99910**, O.Thomas |
| | | | | **Meg 69205**, O.Thomas |
| | | **Udale Gorgie 134345**<br>H.Huddleston | **Ghylan 112514**<br>H.Huddleston | **Tweed 96630**, T.H.Longton, 1981 E.Nat 1st |
| | | | | **Trixie 65888**, W.Huddleston |
| | | | **Udale Blondie 117277**<br>H.Huddleston | **Wardstone Rex 84292**, R.N.Haworth |
| | | | | **Anna 85852**, H.Huddleston |

**Roy 262387**, dog, rough,B&W, born 06-12-2002, CI6 = 0.5% (low, out-cross)
owner: Mrs.S.Cropper

| Parents | Grand-Parents | G.G.-Parents | G.G.G.-Parents | G.G.G.G.-Parents |
|---|---|---|---|---|
| **Mac**<br>**244859**<br><br>J.A.S.Gilchrist<br>MRCVS<br><br>2003 W.Nat 8th | **Joe**<br>**216417**<br>K.R.Donald | **Kep 198049**<br>R.J.Shennan | **Max 171080**<br>J.Brady | **Wull 156904**, D.J.Irvine, 1990 I.Nat 2nd |
| | | | | **Sue 138220**, R.Weatherup |
| | | | **Jed 162697**<br>R.H.Pollock | **York 127630**, J.Paterson, 1983 S.Nat 3th |
| | | | | **Di 126147**, J.Paterson |
| | | **Peg 205521**<br>R.J.Shennan | **Shep 189554**<br>R.J.Shennan | **Tam 181194**, J.H.Logan |
| | | | | **Jen 169930**, R.J.Shennan |
| | | | **Queen 193300**<br>R.Weir | **Pat 145924**, M.Priestly |
| | | | | **Mist 182835**, R.Taylor |
| | **Tess**<br>**233766**<br>K.I.Donald | **Moss 213331**<br>A.S.MacRae | **Glen 145038**<br>J.D.Martin | **Mirk III 120673**, A.S.MacRae, 1985 S.Nat 4th |
| | | | | **Ness 133285**, J.Logan |
| | | | **Jill 192035**<br>A.D.Carnegie | **Craig 148254**, J.H.Harrison, 1990 E.Nat 1st |
| | | | | **Jan 161939**, A.J.Palmer |
| | | **Meg 215003**<br>I.M.Brownlie | **Bill 183017**<br>D.Russell | **Glen 133713**, W.Bremner |
| | | | | **Meg 147858**, D.Russell |
| | | | **Meg 190310**<br>N.M.L.Kidd | **Jix 154800**, M.Watt Jnr. |
| | | | | **Scruff 141530**, I.A.MacMillan |
| **Jess**<br>**248727**<br><br>C.Pickford | **Skye**<br>**232026**<br>S.N.Wilkinson | **Bill 186305**<br>S.N.Wilkinson | **Spot 119958**<br>A.W.Lockhart | **Mac 115688**, J.McGregor |
| | | | | **Vera 93999**, J.H.Wilson |
| | | | **Llangwm Bet 149958**<br>A.W.Lockhart | **Ben 129820**, A.Owen, 1985 IntSu 3th |
| | | | | **Maid 114669**, A.Owen |
| | | **Sue 193831**<br>Mrs.J.A.Elliott | **Glen 143941** J.F.McRobert<br>1990 IntSu 3th | **Mirk III 120673**, A.S.MacRae, 1985 S.Nat 4th |
| | | | | **Nell 131110**, Wm.Wilson |
| | | | **Meg 180204**<br>D.C.Meek | **Lad 136869**, L.N.Watkins |
| | | | | **Peggy 158608**, L.N.Watkins |
| | **Lanehead Haddy**<br>**232433**<br>H.Hallam | **Glen 156384**<br>Miss T.J.Walker | **Rock 130399**<br>J.S.Wilson | **Glen 81435**, W.Sinclair |
| | | | | **Nell 115794**, Wm.Cormack |
| | | | **Trim 133311**<br>A.R.Ashburner | **Dryden Joe 104626**, R.J.Dalziel, 1986 S.Nat 1st |
| | | | | **Trim 101028**, G.Dixon |
| | | **Peg 211433**<br>Miss T.J.Walker | **Glen 143941** J.F.McRobert<br>1990 IntSu 3th | **Mirk III 120673**, A.S.MacRae, 1985 S.Nat 4th |
| | | | | **Nell 131110**, Wm.Wilson |
| | | | **Broadhead Sue 183070**<br>T.A.Temple | **Winder Floyd 153699**, J.Witter |
| | | | | **Wildfell Star 169961**, J.Witter |

# Photo Album

Jim & Shirley's dwelling at Irwell House Farm, Bacup in winter.

A selection of photographs, taken by wildlife and animal artist and photographer Steven Townsend during the winter of 2004/5, mainly showing Jim & Shirley's farm and the surrounding country.

Steven's paintings of the farm (above) and dogs "Rarin' to Go" are just two of his many excellent productions. You can visit The Townsend Gallery at 215 - 233 Accrington Road, Burnley, BB11 5ES, telephone 01282 832060. His website is at www.steventownsend.com

Rarin' to Go.
Painting by Steven Townsend.

Jim and artist/photographer Steven Townsend watch the runs at a trial in 2004.

A sensible Border Collie (or two) is essential at lambing. Bob and Sid help Jim.

Sid to the rescue! A steady, controlled dog is essential on high ground. Use of an unruly one would court disaster.

Ewes are liable to attack dogs when their lambs are very young. A good dog, such as Bob, holds his ground.

Jim and dogs coming home at the end of the day.

Setting off up Deerplay on a cold day.

Glen and Mac watching sheep.

Typical Deerplay weather!

Herdwicks are found all over Lakeland. They are believed to be of Scandinavian origin.

A scene repeated all over Britain's hill country each spring. Note the quality of the stone wall - an invaluable wind break at this altitude.

Tommy Brownrigg, one of the oldest competitors, in typical Cumbrian countryside. His dog has spotted something.

Bob and Sid holding up ewes and lambs.

Dan gathering the Cheviot types, which have taken over from the dark faced horned sheep previously kept, by using a succession of Hill Cheviot rams.

Quad bikes are essential for modern hill farming. The enclosed trailer is for moving ewes and lambs. The reservoir is on the Water Board land where we farm.

The first lamb, born in March, rather too early. However, even very young lambs can survive low temperatures if their tummies are full, and they have protection from wind and driving rain.

Jim in winter garb!

Crossing rough country. Jim with Bob, Mac and Sid in cotton grass.

Holding one sheep for inspection.

Dan and Alf join Jim on the bike.

Shirley with Bob.

Shirley gathering sheep.

Three of Shirley's dogs: Mac, Roy and Lilly.

Shirley with Lilly, Roy, Mac and Bob. Lilly and Roy have both qualified for the 2005 English National in just four months.

A close up of Bob.

A close up of Roy.

# About the Author

Edward Hart is an agricultural journalist and author, with special interests in sheepdogs and upland farming. After grammar school in York, he spent eight years as a farm worker, with a year at the Yorkshire Institute of Agriculture, now Askham Bryan College, York.

He then farmed sheep and cattle in Bilsdale, North Yorkshire, and began writing farming articles for The Northern Echo and Darlington & Stockton Times. In Livestock Farming he initiated the Shepherd of the Year Award. He now contributes regularly to Ark, Country Illustrated, Farmers Guardian, Heavy Horse World, Horse and Hound, The Daily Telegraph and The Yorkshire Post.

A Nuffield Scholarship took him to sheep farms in Iceland as well as throughout Britain. Edward Hart became a full time writer, with books on sheep, sheep dog training, fencing, hedging and drystone walling, besides two titles on shepherds' crooks. He has judged shepherds' crooks at Danby, Patterdale Dog Day and the Great Yorkshire Show. He was a judge in the Bayer/FWAG Hedgerow Competition, and won a Hydro-Agri award for a Country Illustrated feature on hefting.

Edward's two previous books on sheepdogs are Your Sheepdog and its Training and The Sheep Dog: its Work and Training, both written in conjunction with Tim Longton. He is a member of the Swaledale Sheep Breeders Association, "E" District, and is keen on field sports and cricket. He also runs a mail order business for books on sheep, sheep dogs and working horses.

**Titles by Edward Hart:**

Book of the Heavy Horse
The Coloured Horse and Pony
Care and Showing of the Heavy Horse
The Dry Stone Wall Handbook
The Golden Guinea Book of Heavy Horses, Past and Present
Heavy Horses
Heavy Horses: an Anthology
The Heavy Horse
The Harness Horse (with Audrey Hart)
Hedge Laying and Fencing: the Countryman's Art Explained
The Hill Shepherd
Northcountry Farm Animals
Scottish Farm Animals
Pony Trekking
Shepherds' Crooks and Walking Sticks (with David Grant)
Walking Sticks (with Len Parkin)
Your Sheepdog and its Training (with Tim Longton)
The Sheep Dog: its Work and Training (with Tim Longton)
Sheep: a Guide to Management
Shire Horses
Showing Livestock
Sheepkeeping on a Small Scale
Victorian and Edwardian Farming from Old Photographs
Working Dogs (with Audrey Hart)
The Year Round

# Bibliography

Reflections on the Changing Years. Ruth Beckett. 2002.

National Sheepdog Champions: of Britain and Ireland, 1922-1993. E B Carpenter. 1994.

The Blue Riband of the Heather: the Supreme Champions. E B Carpenter. 1989.

A Guide to Sheepdog Trials in Britain and Ireland. Barbara C Collins. 1994.

Border Collies: an Owner's Companion. Iris Combe. 1993.

A Dog's Life in the Dales: Winning Ways with Working Dogs. Katy Cropper, with Barbara Collins. 1992.

It's a Dog's Life. Phil Drabble. 1983.

One Man and His Dog. Phil Drabble. 1989.

I Bought a Mountain. Thomas Firbank. 1940.

Sheepdog Trials. Eric Halsall. 1982.

All in a Lifetime. Edward Hart. 1998.

Hefting in Practice: The Ancient Craft of Grazing the Open Hills. Edward Hart. 2004.

The Hill Shepherd. Edward Hart. 1977.

A Shepherd's Life. W H Hudson. 1949.

Sheepdogs at Work: One Man and his Dogs. Tony Iley. 1978.

Training the Sheep Dog. Thomas Longton and Barbara Sykes. 1997.

The Sheep Dog: Its Work and Training. Tim Longton and Edward Hart. 1989.

Your Sheep Dog and its Training. Tim Longton and Edward Hart. 1969.

Sheep Dogs and their Masters. Herries McCulloch. 1938.

The British Sheepdog. Sydney Moorhouse. 1938.

Owd Bob. Alfred Ollivant. 1898.

I Went A'Shepherding. Richard Perry. 1945.

Understanding Border Collies. Barbara Sykes. 1999.

• For more recent books and videos on sheep and sheepdogs, visit www.workingsheepdog.org